Borrowed Water

LaToya N. Brown

Borrowed Water

© 2007 by LaToya N. Brown
All Rights Reserved

International Standard Book Number
978-0-9794210-1-3

Printed in the United States of America

No part of this publication can be reproduced, stored in a retrieval system, or transmitted in any form or by any means—electronic, mechanical, photocopying, recording or otherwise—without prior permission

Unless otherwise noted all scripture references are from the King James Version of the Bible. The KJV is part of the United States public domain and may be copied without restriction.

FOR INFORMATION:
Soul Water Ministries
P.O. Box 540812
Grand Prairie, Texas 75054-0812
Website: http://www.soulwaters.org

This Book Is Dedicated To

My God

Words could never be enough! Thank you for loving me beyond my fears.

My Children

Tristan, Ashton and JaRicky
Without you there would be no story to tell.

My Friend

Kathy Jimerson
Only heaven will be able to tell of the ways that you have blessed my life.

Fresh dew that comes to a sun parched soul when life has nearly shut the door, when the world has said it's final good-byes and the curtains on the stage of defeat are closing in—ahh Victory.... LaToya Brown

Contents

Foreword..x

Acknowledgements..............................xi

Introduction..1

1. Why I Write..15
2. 1976...31
3. Bald-Headed Charlie..........................54
4. Sticks and Stones................................69
5. Now I Lay Me Down To Weep..........89
6. On My Own.....................................106
7. Encounter of A Lifetime..................129
8. Through The Fire.............................150
9. Change Is Coming............................169
10. If I Could Love Me.........................187

11. Look At Me Now………………………….197

12. Soul Water……………………………....212

If You See Her……………………………....221

About the Author……………………………222

Acknowledgments

My deepest appreciation to …

Tristan, Ashton, and JaRicky, my children—Thank you for your patience. You have been my purpose. You are truly God's gifts to me. Thank you for being patient and believing in me.

My family--Thank you for the lessons learned.

My friends at the YMCA—Thanks for the encouragement and support.

Judge Nancy Robb, my editor--I want to thank you for your willingness to make me look good. We've only known each other for a short while but you've been a blessing. I thank God for bringing you into my life.

Kim Wallace—Thanks you girl for your encouragement. It has always been much appreciated. I have been very fortunate to have you on my side.

Audrenna Easter—Thank you for teaching me how to say, "I love you". You've shown me true beauty.

Sharonda Lewis—Thank you for being by my side for 15 years.

Patsy Palacios—Thanks for all the free trips to school and the grocery store when my car broke down. You were an angel in disguise.

Reva Gray. You've been a sister to me. I appreciate the support you've given through the years.

Madeline Valdez—Thanks for letting me use your van so that I could finish my last semester. It was more than a blessing for you to help me the way that you did. I appreciate you and I love you.

Tammy Williamson, Vickie Smith and all of the volunteers at the Pregnancy Resource Center—You have blessed my life with your grace, unconditional love and true compassion of Jesus Christ. I see you as spiritual mothers and I love you as sisters in Christ.

Alishia Sisk—I have truly appreciated your friendship. I've learned from your candor and "tell it like it is" philosophy. Thank you for the prayers, support and laughter.

Chandreia Owens and Yessenia Evans-Toro. You believed in my vision though you didn't know me. Your support in the past year means more than you could ever understand.

Judi Munoz—I want to thank you for being a real friend. I have loved your crazy personality and contagious laughter. You've blessed my life in so many ways.

Deveise Parker—I'm blessed to have known you. Your friendship has been sweet and filled with the joy of the Lord. I love you girl.

Phil and Kathy Jimerson, my biggest fans--You have truly been an inspiration and you have shown me what it means to be a godly, ambitious, driven woman. I don't know where I would be without your influence and acceptance.

Danika Leeks, my sister in Christ - Girl you have been a Super Blessing. Thank you for encouraging me and helping me with the cover of this book.

Antonio Jeter, my friend--Thank you for challenging me to do less talking and more writing. If it hadn't been for you, I'd still be telling everyone about this "great" book that I was going to write someday. Thank you for holding me accountable and inspiring me to finish what I started. You've helped me move beyond being a "woman of many words" to being a "woman of many results."

Jackson Ehioguh. God knows what you need when you need it. You've been more than a blessing to me. Thank you for your support, strong belief in me, putting your money where you mouth is and allowing me to use your office so that I could finish this book.

Foreword

Experiences and circumstances do not define us; they explain us.

Many people don't understand this and they allow experiences to dictate their destiny.

I've met many of those people; they have a "victim mentality." Woe is me, poor me, feel sorry for me, everybody owes me, I can't help myself. They don't want or need help; they want a handout. Trust me when I say…I've met many of these folks.

I worked with teen parents for years. That is when and how I met LaToya. At the age of fourteen she was the single mother of two, living from place to place, and little to no prospects of a future or rising above the welfare system she had grown up in. She embodied what we view as failure.

The first day I met privately with her we played stare out, only she stared at the floor. If you want to know what broke the ice you can read the chapter, Experience of a Lifetime.

After that day it would be years of building a relationship of trust, but looking back I'm so glad I had the opportunity to help unlock the wounded heart of this beautiful soul. What a tremendous gift she is to this generation and to women of all diversity.

I had the honor of walking beside her throughout the high school years when graduation looked impossible. I was there when she graduated from community college; I was there when she graduated with a Bachelors degree and I applauded her when she graduated with a Masters Degree.

But it was the day she asked Christ to become her Lord and real teacher that I treasure the most. That was when I knew the sky was the limit! I knew she was truly going places bigger than we either could imagine!

LaToya had a part to play in all of this. There was a lot of hard work to do and she did it. And somewhere along the way she stopped believing in what she couldn't do, she stopped believing in what others said about her, and she found her identity and her own voice.

Today she is using that voice and what she has learned to help those who will listen.

Her story may be your story; it may be someone else's story. But what she shares is candid, honest, and written to bring healing to others. To open her life and walk back through those years of pain reveals her deep commitment to helping other women.

I loved and respected her as a girl; I admire her as a young woman.

She is a tribute to the real American dream when God is the author.

Thank you, LaToya for allowing me to write this foreword.

Kathy Henigan Jimerson

Introduction

"Write, Toya, Write! Write about your life, your struggles, your dreams, your hopes, your disappointments, and your victory. That's what your name means! You are "The Victorious One," right? Are you victorious?

Then tell them. Tell them how to overcome. Tell them how you were victorious. Just write about your life and what has brought you to rest your story on these pages."

When I first decided to write this book, many things came to mind. Who will I speak to? What will I discuss? What kind of impact do I want to make? My life is more than just a few words written between the pages of a book.

It is the depiction of how I as an abused, teenage mother turned my struggles, hardships and failures into success.

It is the ultimate demonstration of God's power and love that worked in my life.

There is so much to say about my life and there are so many of you who need to hear the hope my story will bring.

Have you ever felt unwanted? Have you ever felt like you were rejected the moment you entered this world? Felt as if a red, "rejected" sign had been stamped on your birth certificate? From that moment you've moved from one scene in your life to the next only to replay the previous scene over and over—leaving you feeling dizzy and inadequate?

Have you ever felt like no matter how hard you tried, the result always ended up the same—rejected?

I'm sure many of you have felt like this at some point in your life. It's the exact point when you question your existence and purpose. We may all have a story to write about the unwelcome friend that invades our thoughts, bombards our conscience and alienates our soul.

This unwelcome rejection finds its way into our lives and sets up camp.

While many of you may be able to say, "Hey, I'm over that," many of you, including myself have been married to rejection. We know what it feels like to be the outcast: the one not wanted. It was all that I knew. In my world, "accepted" was the stranger

Writing this book was difficult. In order to help you I had to first help me. I had to realize that there was still a lot of healing that needed to take place. I had to revisit my past and confront the pain that I thought I buried.

The pain I never wanted to see or feel again. The past was a place I left a long time ago and vowed to never return.

I can't help you find your way to freedom if I fail to face yesterday once and for all. I had to be willing to step back into the past--uncover all the hidden lies that had been tormenting me—confront the wounds and begin the road to healing.

Writing this book would mean that I'd have to be a little girl all over again, so that you can understand the woman I am. I haven't always been courageous.

For many years I was a hidden coward-- putting on a bold front for the world as an attempt protect myself from hurt. I told myself, "all was well." I lied to myself. My past was influencing my present and robbing my future.

I had become an expert at hiding the pain. I wanted to world to see that I had arrived unharmed. Although, I did "make it" there were still parts of my heart that needed to heal. The sooner I overcame this realization the better my life would be.

Over the years I developed the habit of being in control. I had been hurt so many times that I couldn't distinguish between love and pain. I made up my mind that I was the only one who could and would protect LaToya. As long as I could keep people at arms length then the better off I'd be.

I had the choice to either be in control or be controlled.

Being in control meant protecting my heart and body from pain. I exercised control over my children, my friends and my education. Somewhere in the back of my mind I'd resolved that no one could be trusted. Everyone was out to get me. I was going to take care of myself--at all cost.

The danger in having this attitude is that I deceived myself about reality. Nothing was in my control, nor had it ever been and that's what I feared the most. There was a world out there that had hurt me and could hurt me again and there was absolutely nothing that I could do about it.

My life seemed to be surrounded with the fate of always being wounded—always being forgotten.

I fooled myself into thinking that I was the only one who was going to determine if or how anyone would ever abuse, hurt, neglect or reject me again. I didn't realize that I had no control over the pain that would come my way.

My entire life had been filled with one disappointment after another. I eventually gave up on the idea of ever being loved and accepted.

I was so blinded by control that I hadn't realized that I was rejecting myself before anyone else had the opportunity. It was easier for me to hate the person that looked back at me when I looked in the mirror. I finally saw what I thought everyone else saw: A poor black girl who had too many kids, a girl who had no future, a girl who was ugly and fat, a girl who would never know love.

As I observed what I saw in the mirror and accepted the lie as fact, the blows from others didn't hurt as bad. I was numb from my self-inflicted pain. I was tired of being hurt and talked about. I was tired of being the brunt of everyone's jokes. I was tired.

However, there was a part of me that refused to succumb to the lies spoken. There is one thing about me that was for sure. That one thing-- is that I refused to have a quitter attitude. Regardless of the pain I experienced, I wouldn't let the world win over my life. I was determined to be more than what I or anyone else had to say.

If I was ever going to overcome my past and be victorious in my future, then I had some decisions to make. I could remain the same and live my life in the shadows of others or take a risk, venture out into the familiar places and fight back.

I needed to leave the past behind me and take one step at a time towards the future that I wanted to create.

I barricaded my feelings about the past behind a wall called "forgotten" in an attempt to escape the fire without the stench of smoke. I buried my fears deep inside. I believed that I'd moved beyond yesterday. "Forgive and forget" was my philosophy. After all, our yesterdays are not part of our tomorrows, right?
Wrong.

The buried pain resurfaced with a vengeance. I couldn't hide anymore. The walls had to come down and the fears had to be released. I needed to be free from the past so that I could look back and see just how far I'd come. I surrounded myself with enormous brick walls in my human way of saying "it hurt."

What I feared saying then--I'm saying now. It hurt to be abused. It hurt to be talked about. It hurt to be laughed at. It hurt to be rejected. It hurt to be hated because of the color of my skin. It hurt to be me. As a grown mother of three children –it still hurt. No matter how much I tried to hide the pain with degrees, laughter or success, it still hurt.

I realized that it's okay to feel. It's okay to voice my hurt, my pain and my fear of rejection even as an adult. I assumed that my age meant I had outgrown those childhood fears and had forgotten the pain. I've felt the sting of rejection and I can't declare that it doesn't affect me today. I'd be lying to you and I'd be lying to myself.

Regardless of how hard I tried to hide, there was a timid, broken, beat down little black girl screaming to experience a life without pain. Wanting to experience a life filled with love--whatever that meant, I wanted to be free.

Life is the good, the bad, the ugly… and everything in between. You don't know how it starts or how it ends--It just is. Or is it?

Living is supposed to be an event that leads us to our destinies and fulfills our dreams. For me "living" was wounding territory. With every breath I breathed, it reminded me of my existence. It reminded me of my failures and of my pain. It reminded me of the injustice, abuse, and rejection that I suffered.

I was a child with a broken heart, shattered dreams: unwanted --craving love, attention, and appreciation. I was always wondering WHY? Why was I born? Why was I black—ugly or bald-headed? Why did everybody talk about me? Why did the world hate me? These questions went unanswered for a long time.

I used to wonder if God was present. I questioned His love for me. I wondered if He heard my cries for someone to love me. If He did care and if He did love me, why didn't He stop the pain? He could've stepped in and stopped the abuse.

He should've stepped in when my future was being molested!

I wished that He 'd rescued me when thoughts of suicide tormented me. I often wondered where God was at the most crucial points in my life.

At first glance, I could honestly say I had no idea where God was or why He didn't rescue me. The least He could do was answer my questions. It seemed as if God had ignored my cries. However, when I looked back on the cracked soil of my past, after the dust had settled — I saw him.

I saw Him, in all of His power and love, take every hurt, pain, disappointment and use it—to use me! He's using my past, my pain and my failures to demonstrate the hope and victory that you too can experience when you surrender.

Giving my life to him was more than just a decision. It was a life-saving moment.

Since I was a little girl everyone who had control over my life abused it, mistreated it and neglected it. I wasn't any different. I did the same thing. I too abused, neglected and mistreated my life. It was all I knew. It was my "normal."

God has done so much in my life that I can hardly begin to tell it all. When trials get the best of me or past mistakes seek to whisper failure in my ears, I'm forced to reflect on the journey and remember how far I've come. And as I look back, I remember just how far God has brought me.

There were times when I wanted to give up. It almost seemed like the right thing to do. There were times when giving up would've made those around me happy. I would've fallen prey to the old saying "I told you so."

What kept me from giving up? I didn't give up because I'm not a quitter. I've never had a quitter attitude. I hate defeat. I made up my mind a long time ago that nothing would defeat me and no one would tell me what I could or couldn't do because they didn't create me. I've always been a conqueror and I always will be.

This book is not a "feel good" session, nor is it a tragic glimpse into my life. This book has been written to show you that, through tragedy, pain and poor choices, we can still overcome. This book is for anyone who has suffered rejection, abuse, and neglect. It's also for those who suffer from the consequences of self-inflicted wounds from bad decisions you've made. Life is too complicated for me to deliver empty promises through this paper and ink.

I've rested my story on these pages to help you see beyond your pain: no longer being tormented by what could've been should've been or what you wish had never been. This book is about challenging you to envision the hope that lies ahead.

This book is to the young girl whose voice has been silenced through molestation, rape and abuse; it's to the single mom who wants to give up because you feel like you can never get it right; it's to the hurting woman who regrets the decisions she's made and is desperate for relief.

This book is to all of you who want to find your way out of the mess.
Nothing is final until you give up.

Proverbs 27: 7

*He who is full loathes honey,
But to the hungry even
what is bitter tastes sweet.*

Water heals the wounds
Slowly releases the soul
Water nourishes the blood
Soothing the veins in which it flows...

Water embraces the truth
Purification releases the path
Water redeems lost time
Of treasures buried in the past...

Water quenches the thirst
Spiritually revives the spirit
Water renews the hope
To escape life-draining prison...

Water purifies yesterday
Water cleanses the pain
Water hopes for better
Of pain to never feel again

Water is free

~ Chapter 1 ~

Why I Write

On Sunday, December 17, 2006, God spoke to me about the title to this book. I prayed for a title that would be intriguing and inviting. I asked God for the right title that would catch the attention of every reader. I wanted the title to impact you just as much as the book would.

I was being more than patient because this book needed to be personal, and most importantly it needed to be real.

As I was recalling my childhood and all that had happened to get me to this point, I couldn't help but to remember the specific moments that altered my life.

Borrowed Water

I recalled the times that I had to borrow water, the times that I suffered abuse or even the time I was molested. It's been difficult for me to reflect on yesterday. The pain had been buried deep enough so that I wouldn't have to feel it again.

I realized that my yesterday is part of the story that tells of triumphs, hurdles jumped and dreams realized. Without the past I wouldn't be writing this book and I wouldn't have the opportunity to help you recover from yours.

You may be wondering what Borrowed Water has to do with my life. Let me tell you and let me tell you about why it's important to me.

Water has significance. When I was a child, we frequently had to borrow water from our neighbors. Our water was off more than it was on. We lacked the water to drink, cook with or to take a bath.

To say that it was embarrassing would be an understatement. It was death. We were the laughing stock of the neighborhood from kids and adults alike.

Why I Write

We lived in one of the dirtiest houses on the block. Everybody talked about us, especially the kids in the neighborhood. Sadly, the adults had just as much to say. I don't know which one hurt the most: the words from the kids who didn't know any better or the words from the adults who should've known better.

No matter how much we hated to borrow water, our thirst and the hand of my Mom against our backs made us do it. We often tried to wait until the sun went down or the kids went into their houses before we took the embarrassing journey into the neighborhood. There would be times when we'd wait so long to borrow water that our tongues would stick to the roofs of our mouths.

We hated to ask (beg) for water because of the humiliation and because of the embarrassment we knew was coming.

Even though we hated it, our thirst would win and there we'd go carrying our empty milk jugs and two-liter coke bottles in the Texas heat to inconvenience another neighbor. Weather in Texas would get so hot you could fry chicken on the sidewalk. I felt every degree on my back. It wasn't odd to have temperatures over 102 degrees. The heat made our trip harder and longer.

Several neighbors would let us know that we were getting on their nerves. They'd let out a huge sigh, tell us "no" and close the door in our faces. We couldn't let that stop us though. We were thirsty and we were on a mission to fill our empty bodies with the nourishment that we thirsted after. We kept asking until someone gave in.

At times they'd let us get water from their kitchen faucet and other times they'd only allow us to get water from the water hose in the front yard. It depended on who they were and how they felt that day. It was always nice to go inside. The cool air gave us a break from the scorching heat.

We didn't care about the structure just as long as we were able to get water. While we filled up the containers we'd slip our mouths under the water hose to guzzle a drink before we took the long walk back home--which always seemed longer with heavy water jugs. There was nothing more satisfying than a cool drink of water on a hot Texas day.

My first name should have been "empty" and my last name "bottle", because that's how I felt. I was an empty bottle--a bottle that was of no use. I was empty and I was thirsty. I was thirsty for encouraging, loving water--the water that's carried on the tongues of those in my life. Oh, how I needed the "water" of kind words, hugs and support. I thirsted for affirmations and "atta-girls"

My thirst turned to dehydration. Once dehydration settled in, desperation shortly followed. Dehydration left me desperate for water from any stranger's water hose and my family's kitchen faucet. I drank all I could get in view of the fact that I didn't know when my next drink would come.

Water is the essence of life. Without this resource, death is eminent. We can't live more than one week without water. It keeps us alive. It enables our body to function and grow. Without water tree roots shrivel, green grass fades to a crispy brown, and the foundation of homes becomes unstable.

All water isn't healthy. All water doesn't bring life. Dirty water carries disease, dysfunction and death. Contaminated water hinders growth and slows the flow of life.

Because I didn't have the water I needed, I borrowed water from others. My thirst forced me to borrow water from the lives of others. I drank my destiny from their fountains. I drank and I drank.

When they said that I would never be anything--I took a drink. When they told me that I was as dumb as a box of rocks--I took a drink. When I was molested–I took a drink. When I was raped-- I took a drink. I took a drink every time something was spoken. I absorbed everything that was said about me. Those words became my identity.

I borrowed my dreams, my goals, my future and my identity from strangers' water hoses. Unfortunately, the stranger's hoses weren't the only source from which I drank. I most often took a drink from kitchen faucets of family members.

I drank the water of their life experiences. I allowed them to pour their judgment, lies, ridicule, destruction and rejection into my empty bottle.

I hated drinking their water, but I was thirsty. I didn't have a choice. I needed water regardless of the source. I lived this way for many years. I hated my life in the most terrible way. I wanted to kill myself. I embraced the idea that the world without me would be a world less one 'idiot'. Death couldn't come soon enough.

I wanted the water that I thirsted after to drown me so I could escape the pain. In my opinion, there was nothing worth living for. I wanted to die and thought about it often. Fear of the unknown kept me from committing suicide and pain of the known pushed me towards it. I wished that life—my life—could be different. I didn't know how much more I could take.

As a child, I remember my family telling me being that I was ugly; too black, had no common sense, and was as dumb as a box of rocks. I learned early on that if the family who was supposed to love me, felt this way, then the world was either going to shelter me or add to the pain. My family's version of love distorted my purpose and existence.

I accepted the negative comments as fact. I lived up to the low expectations many times. I unconsciously allowed those life-destroying words to dictate my behavior. A part of me wanted to fight and a part of me believed what was being said. "I could prove them wrong" I thought. So, I'd fight a little harder to break free only to find myself back in the same pit of despair: still desperate and thirsty.

From a young age I thought little of myself. My pain and insecurities pushed me into looking for love in the wrong places and with the wrong people. My search for validation pushed me into the arms of another kid; ultimately leaving me with three children by the time I was 17.

I was thirsty for affection and love from any place that I could find it. It never came. Self-hatred was my best friend and regret was my constant companion.

People called me names. I lost friends. People told me I would never amount to anything. Based on statistics, I was at-risk of dropping out of school, being on welfare for the rest of my life, and never attain higher levels of education. I was a loser and I felt like one.

Were they right? Was I as dumb as a box of rocks to get pregnant three times? Did I lack common sense if I thought I was being loved through having sex?

I spent many years searching for someone to love me. I wished someone would've looked beyond the cute face and loved me for me. Because of this search for love and acceptance, I made so many poor choices that could have ended my life or ruined it.

I was mad at God for a long time. Did he hear me on the night I was molested? Did he hear me the night I was raped? Did he hear, Toya? Did He notice that I hadn't stopped crying since the day

I was born? I'd get knocked to the ground with a blow to my soul and before I could recuperate and stand on my feet another round of contaminated water would shove me back down. God needed to do something and He needed to do it fast.

    I was drowning in a river of deception and I didn't know how to swim. I was tired of fighting. I didn't know it at the time but change was coming. No matter what I went through in my childhood, adolescence or adulthood, I survived it all. No matter what happened back then I'm still here. I'm still here to tell my story – and to tell it boldly.

I'm stronger

I'm courageous

I'm victorious

I survived.

    How did I do it?

    I surrendered. I gave up control. I let it all go. I let go of all the pain caused by my family. I let go of all the lies spoken over me. Letting go of the past meant that I could embrace my new future and all the hope that lay ahead for me.

I'd be lying to you if I told you that it was all me. I didn't have enough power to change my life. When I say that I surrendered my life, I meant that I surrendered my life to God. Only He could undo the damage that had been done. I needed a supernatural power to rescue me.

It wasn't until I met Jesus Christ, the real source of water, that my life changed. He filled my life with fresh, soul-cleansing water and I have never been the same.

His water flushed out the mud, parasites and slime that had previously saturated my life. It reversed disease, overturned dysfunction and eliminated death. It healed my wounds.

His water caused my roots to grow deep, and the green pastures of my spirit to flourish. He restored me in ways that I didn't know I could be restored. I'm no longer that lonely, hurting little girl. I am wiser, stronger and more determined than ever. I can and will be victorious in life.

Are you thirsty? Dehydrated? Are you borrowing water? Whose fountain have you been drinking from? Who's told you that you're nothing? Is it a water hose or a kitchen faucet? Have you taken a drink of rejection and neglect? Have you drunk from the well of rape, molestation, and abuse? Has it caused you to refuse water entirely?

Water is supposed to be the nourishment that enables us to fulfill our destinies, achieve our goals and realize our dreams. But for many of you, borrowing water has become your existence. With every drink you drink, you're reminded of what each drop represents: rejection, lies, deception or abuse.

Of all the watered-down words people spoke in my life, they could not compare to the one word that would change my life forever. The powerful word of 'belief' showed me that the environment from which I came was not who I was, nor did it indicate where I was going.

My hope was more than just an oasis in the desert. It was real and it was in reach. I could taste it. A small drop of victory was placed on my tongue and I was thirsty for more.

Belief welled up on the inside and made me realize that I was the only person who had the authority to determine my direction. I realized that having a bad start in life did not predict the ending. I could either wallow in my self-pity or push back. I had to fight back. I had to fight against the strikes against me and prove to myself that I could be anything I set my mind and heart to become. If it's gonna be, it's up to me--and God.

It was God who helped me believe that I could move beyond my past and refuse to allow it to rob me of the tomorrow that I was to create. I was tragically disappointed before I had a chance to live. However, I didn't allow those disappointments to steal my sense of purpose—permanently!

We didn't ask to be born, abused, neglected, or mistreated. No child does! No human does! We couldn't choose our family. We have no control over the environment in which we were born. There is one thing that I have learned over the years-- It's not where you start that matters, it's where you finish. Regardless of where your drinking started, you determine where it ends!

Ultimately, life is about decisions: the decision to live on water poured out by every passerby or the decision to live above the criticism.

I believe that you can recover from life decisions once made or the ones that were made for you that altered your life. You can't change what happened yesterday, but you can change your tomorrow.

I invite you to take this journey of healing with me. As you read each word on these pages and begin to remember past situations that caused you to pick up this book, I give you permission to cry, to scream, and to let it all go. This book is not just about me. It's not just about you. It's about us. It's about healing and for the rest of our days it will be about winning.

I choose to win today. I choose to be victorious. I choose to fly high above the circumstances, complaints and confusion that tormented me for years. I choose to fly high so that

I fly high enough to see what God has in store for me.

Why do I write?

I write so that you can trash the residue from the past and begin to create your new future—today. I invite you to see how I overcame all the struggles, hardships and abuse that invaded my territory. I write so that you may see my victory and begin believing that God will do the same for you. I write to release my own pain of yesterday, and I write to heal my tomorrow.

So, pour out all of your borrowed pain, disappointment, bad decisions, destructive comments and hopelessness in a container called "no more" and be encouraged to live the life that God has for you.

Be stronger.

Be courageous

Be victorious.

Be free.

Shhhh...Do you hear that?

Here comes another soul

Tiptoeing through eternity

Forging towards this life unknown

Perfectly slipping into a generation

Where only God could ever know

The destination and life

Of this rejected, outcast soul

Shhh... Do you hear that?

The color of her skin hated

The whine of her cries ignored

Her life decisions quietly debated

Crush her, destroy her

Molest her God-inspired soul

Ensure that rejection controls her

Make sure she's never whole

Whispers of baby cries tiptoe across my soul – search

me, find me, free me, so that I may live

Shhhh...Here she comes

~ Chapter 2 ~

1976

"It's a girl." August 03, 1976-- The day I was born. The day I entered the world as LaToya Nicole Marcus: 7lbs, 6oz. This is the day I took a journey through the womb of an unmarried, teenage girl.

This was the blistering, August day doctors and nurses ushered me into the world never knowing what was to become of this little black baby born in a county hospital. I wonder if they even cared. I wonder if anyone cared.

Does anyone ever look at a newborn baby and consider what life they will lead? Do they ever think about who this little person is or soon to become?

I was born with several strikes against me: I was black, I had asthma and I was fatherless. I was born a few feet behind the starting line: a few feet behind the white, the fortunate, the males, the healthy and those with a daddy.

There is a part of me that wishes I could've known what that day was like. Was I cute and cuddly, fat or bubbly? Was I planned or was I a dim reality in the life of a black, teenage Mom? I know I wanted to be wanted.

I would like to think that champagne bottles were popped and "it's a girl" cigars were passed around to family and friends joining in to celebrate this awesome arrival. My life experience would soon tell me that my entry was far less glamorous.

I'm sure I was cuddled and kissed like every other child on the maternity ward that day, soon to leave the hospital with my future left to chance. Who dreamed for me? Who hoped for me? On August 3, 1976 did anyone care — for me?

1976

Who dreams for babies? Who takes a newborn infant into their arms and visualizes the life this child will live or the lives this baby might change? Did they wonder if I'd become a successful lawyer, doctor, teacher or perhaps just a dropout or teen parent living on welfare? Was I viewed as a welcome addition to the family or just another mouth to feed?

Did anyone look at me and count more than my fingers and toes? Did they count the person I would one day become?

I doubt it. Somehow, this part of the birth experience is lost in the blue "it's a boy" wreaths that neatly hang from maternity room doors and the pink booties that cradle the feet of newborn girls. These adornments distract the world from thinking about the days and years ahead.

Ten women in a single-room hospital ward gaining respite from labor, watching as each nurse, clothed in crisp-white, uniforms with matching hats, pace between each patient, giving some medicine and sanitary napkins, accurately describes the county hospital experience.

"Roll 'em in and roll 'em out."

"Too many to cuddle and too many to care."

I could begin this journey of my life telling you about the great family I had, but I won't. I won't tell you that because it isn't true.

So, here I was, cute, as a button —I'm sure; ill prepared for the life I would soon experience-- hate.

While I'll never know the details of that day I do know what happened in the days and years that followed. I know that Hell had a mission and I was the target. Abuse is what followed. You name it and I experienced it. The abuse was subtle and at times blatant. I'll tell you more about it in a later chapter

Shortly after my birth I was taken to 622 SW 15th street where I would spend the next 12 years of my life.

My Grandmomma's house was the biggest house in the neighborhood. Everything that happened in or near that house was magnified just

1976

because it was so big, dirty and yellow. It was as if life took a highlighter and painted the house to let the world know just how filthy it was. It felt as if our poverty, inadequacies and lack were broadcast throughout the neighborhood.

I was the second child of eight. My sister, who was born two years after me, died of bacterial meningitis when she was eight months old. That left seven of us. Add this number to the countless number of cousins that lived with us off and on and you would have a house full of people. Needless to say there were a lot of kids in the home.

My oldest sister and my brother, who's a year younger than me, shared the same father. My last five siblings shared the same father. I fell somewhere in between. I didn't share a daddy with anyone. I certainly didn't have a relationship with him.

There was one person in my life whom I was crazy about. That man was my Granddaddy. I loved the heck out of my Granddaddy and He loved me. I could do no wrong in his sight. He was my protector.

My Granddaddy was a large man, with a pigged-nose and a big stomach, which was probably a result of his drinking and of course his eating. At night I would climb into the bed with him and watch his stomach move up and down, as if it was a balloon that inflated and deflated with each breath that he took. It was a funny sight to watch.

I didn't care that he had a big stomach. I liked being next to his stomach. I would nestle close to his chest, smelling the faint scent of Crown Royale on his breath and fall asleep listening to his gurgling snores. Resting in his arms was the safest place to be. In his arms there were no worries. It was a safe place to rest my little five-year old head.

When he was around there were no worries about food nor were there worries about love. As long as he had breath in his body, I knew there would be love in mine. It wasn't that he told me. He didn't have to. He showed me.

1976

My Granddaddy stored food in the closet in my Grandmamma's room. It was always filled to the brim with food and goodies. There were five gallon buckets full of corn meal, flour and sugar. Cakes and cookies lined the rows on the shelves.

Growing up during the Great Depression instilled him with a goal. He made sure that food was always in the house. His provision spelled love for me. His provision was his love for the family. That's how I knew he loved me. He always provided.

He also kept a five-gallon bucket on top of his bookshelf headboard so he'd have plenty of room to place the bucket of candy and gallon of whisky. The bucket was filled with Brach's candy. Every Brach's flavor imaginable was in that bucket: caramel, Neapolitan-Coconut chews, fruity nougat, bubble-gum, peppermints, cinnamon and butterscotch disks. Eating from that bucket was like eating from heaven.

My Granddaddy had a profound love for sugar. He loved it so much that if he didn't have any food, he'd eat sugar cubes. Whatever he ate, he made sure he shared it with me. If he ate sugar cubes, then I ate sugar cubes. The cubes were as dry as cotton at first, but once saliva coated them, they would melt in my mouth. They weren't as good as the butterscotch disk and coconut chews but they worked.

I was my Granddaddy's favorite or at least I would like to think so. I was the only child he would allow to get candy from the bucket without asking. My cousins, brothers and sisters would beg me to get candy from him. I loved the feeling of them begging me. I felt like I had control. It gave me power. Unfortunately, that would be the only power I would have for a long time.

I find it odd that my Granddaddy was the only person that I remember before the age of five. No one else mattered I suppose. My world revolved around him; so much so that I do remember my Mom giving me a whooping because my Granddaddy gave me some corn chips.

1976

One day I remember standing in the entryway of my Granddaddy's room eating stale corn chips that he had just given me. I saw my Mom coming towards me but I didn't think anything of it. When she reached me she pelted me on my back with her heavy hand. She hit me so hard the chips I had in my hand fell to the floor and the ones that I was chewing jumped from my mouth, coated with slobber and slid down my shirt.

"Don't be taking stuff from him" she screamed

The pound of her hands against my back stung as if a million ants had bitten me. It took me a moment to cry. I let out one of those silent cries until my voice came back.

"Shut up and don't be taking stuff from him" was all she said.

She grabbed me by the hand and dragged me into another room where I cried off the sting that I still felt on my back. I knew I couldn't go back into my Granddaddy's room that day. I knew I'd get another whooping.

From that one incident, hate was conceived in my heart for her. There may have been incidences prior to this one that I can't recollect, but this one stood out in my mind. I didn't like that woman. As a matter of fact I hated her. At five years old—I hated her.

She blamed me for someone else's actions. I got a whooping for what an adult did. He gave me the corn chip, but I was at fault for eating them. At that moment I drank the lie that I was to blame for the actions of others, especially adults.

I remember thinking "dang, it was just corn chips. Why did she care if I ate a few corn chips – stale corn chips at that?" I wondered what it was about my Granddaddy giving me something that bothered her so much. Why did I get a whooping for being loved?

My Granddaddy became ill shortly after that incident. Time seemed to have stopped when he went into the hospital. I didn't know what happened at the time. I was told that he was sick and that he had to spend some time in the hospital.

1976

Even though the adults tried to keep everything a secret from the kids, I was pretty sharp. I understood their conversations. I understood that my Granddaddy had stomach cancer and that he had to have surgery. I understood that they didn't know whether or not he'd survive.

I didn't say anything while they discussed what was happening. I just listened.

I knew something was wrong the night my aunt came over. My aunt was a licensed vocational nurse or what we call an LVN. She worked the night shift at the hospital. For her to come over at night meant that something was wrong, because she should've been at work.

The moment she walked into the room, I already knew. I knew my Granddaddy was dead.

I stood in the doorway between my Granddaddy's room and the room where my Mom and Grandmamma were in. I waited to hear the words that would change my life forever.

"Willie, died in surgery," she tried to whisper.

Borrowed Water

My heart dropped. I could feel it plummet into the pit of my stomach. I was so shocked that I couldn't even cry. I knew that I was going to hear those words but I didn't expect them to hurt so badly.

I was unsure about what this all meant for me but my protector was gone. I could no longer run to him for safety—it had just been stripped from me. When my granddaddy died, my whole world fell apart. He was the only one who loved me. I was alone. I was scared.

After he died things in the entire house changed in lightening speed. When he died – the food died with him. I don't know why or how that happened, but it did. It seemed like it happened overnight. One day we were doing well and the next day we were starving.

One day I was loved and protected and the next day I was hungry and abused. The closet that once contained the food for my body became the instrument of deprivation and abuse.

1976

When we did something "bad" or got into any type of trouble, we'd get a whooping. Momma would lock us in the closet for long periods of time. It seemed like we were in the closet forever. Too often we stayed in the closet until we fell asleep. Staying in the closet wasn't all that bad when it was full of food. I would quietly eat the snack cakes and chips that lay on the shelves.

At an early age I figured out how to con my Mom. I thwarted her plans for punishment by crying for my Granddaddy when she threatened to put me in the closet. I guess she'd feel bad for what she was about to do, so instead of putting me in the closet, she'd give me a single-serve pecan pie and let me go outside to play. It was deceitful but it was delightful. At that point I didn't care anymore.

Shortly thereafter, the closet no longer contained the scent of individual pecan pies or windmill cookies nicely stacked one upon another. It smelled of dead rats and roach dander. Dust had settled onto the shelves, illuminating the place where food was once placed.

Borrowed Water

Rings had formed where canned peaches, green beans and corn once stood. Square etches of dirt from the boxed cooking starch took its rightful place along the shelf. All those markings left behind small reminders of the nutrition and safety the closet, my home, my life once knew.

My Granddaddy loved me and his love was the last time that I would ever feel the unconditional love of a man. My life would never be the same without him.

My Grandmamma was a different story. Not that she was mean or didn't love me. She was different than my Granddaddy, so she showed me her love in a different way. My Granddaddy spoiled me and she taught me. She was like me in a lot of ways. She had deficits. She was deaf, she was raised without a parent and her skin was almost as dark as mine. I took a real interest in this lady that I called Grandmamma. We had a lot in common. I clung to her after my Granddaddy died. I wanted to know her like I knew him. She seemed to have a strength that couldn't be defined.

1976

My Grandmamma was mixed with Black and Hispanic. Her skin was dark, sun-kissed maroon with no wrinkles in sight. Her long, salt-and-pepper colored hair flowed down her back. She resembled the drawing of a Pueblo Indian when her hair was braided.

The veins in her hands looked like rivers flowing, one connecting to another

When she was in the 6th grade, her stepmother put rat poison in her milk. It didn't kill her, but it caused her to go deaf. She had to drop out of school because she could no longer hear. She adapted by reading lips. The only way we could talk to her was through slow speaking and hand gestures. But we learned how to communicate regardless of the obstacles.

What I remember most about her was her faith in God. I watched her time after time take all the money she had and send it to some televangelist who promised her a healing cloth in exchange for money. She'd receive things in the mail that ranged from handkerchiefs that supposedly possessed the powers of healing or she'd get a tube of oil that was "from the holy land". I'm sure those things were scams but she didn't care about that. She cared about getting all that God had for her, which wasn't much since she lived on disability. But she gave and gave believing that what the pastor's said would come true.

    I loved to sit at her feet while she told stories of her childhood and the Bible. She had a way with stories that captured my attention. She spoke with confidence—always careful to describe each event in grave detail. It was at her feet that I learned more about her. I saw her strength and faith shine through her smile.

    It was through her stories that I learned of her abuse at the hands of her stepmother. I knew of her life struggles and disappointments. I knew what brought her to the place that caused her to believe in God regardless of who the messenger was.

    I learned a lot from watching her. I learned that people lie and they will use you to get what they want. I learned that people who were sent by

1976

God to love and protect you could be the same people through whom abuse could come. There was a hidden lesson for me in what my Grandmamma did. . Her faith wasn't completely locked into the televangelist's theories. It was in God. Her relationship with God was stronger than I realized.

One night, my grandmother was babysitting my brother, my cousin and me. We knew she could only read lips and therefore could not hear us if we were to be a little inappropriate. After making sure her back was turned, we started cussing up a storm. We said every word ever been invented.

I even stood up and danced to each curse word. We cussed so much-- it started to sound like a song – all the words flowing together. It was poetry in motion. I was the lookout. It was my job to make sure that we didn't get caught, not by my Grandmamma, but by whoever would come into the room.

All of a sudden--like a synchronized clock— she slowly turned her head around like Linda Blair in the Exorcist. The slow movement of her head told me she knew exactly what we were doing. She didn't say a word. She didn't have to. I knew she knew God and He must've opened His big mouth and told on us.

We whispered in a panic to each other, slapping each other on the arm "she can hear," "she was lying to us," "she can hear."

We were shocked and convinced that she could hear, even if her hearing was on another level. She heard something. She had my attention.

There is a lot I observed about my Grandmamma and her faith in God. Her faith in God would later be the foundation I needed to get through the rough times ahead. Besides the Bible stories she recounted, there was something in her life telling me she really knew God.

It wasn't that she watched Christian television or read her Bible everyday. It was the real experiences with the supernatural that convinced me. Let me explain.

There were times when my Mom had to go to the laundry mat or run an errand and she'd leave

1976

my brother, my cousin and me with my Grandmamma. There were two occasions when she had to keep us at night. We'd all go into her bedroom, lock all the doors in the house and close the two doors that led to her room. At some point during the night, my grandmamma got up off of her bed and went to the door.

Now, there were four of us in the room and only three of us could hear. There were three doors that led to the inside of the house and we (those who could hear) never heard anyone knock on any of those doors.

We didn't hear anyone knock on the inside doors, cause it would mean that someone managed to get inside the house. But she'd get up and open the door, with us clinging to her side—afraid. When she opened the door there was a man clothed in white standing in the kitchen.

The light in the kitchen was so bright that I had to hold my hands close to my face in order to even get a glimpse. The light was so bright that it burned my eyes. I realized that the kitchen light wasn't on. The light was coming from this man. The man standing in my grandma's kitchen illuminated the whole room.

    I was only able to see his silhouette. This stranger and my Grandmamma started talking to each other, but I couldn't hear what either one of them were saying. The man nodded his head, took off his hat, tipped towards her as the old men used to do in western movies and then he turned to walk out. My grandmother gestured us back into the room, closed the door and sat back down on the bed as if nothing happened. This strange phenomenon happened twice.

    I had a relationship with God since I was a little girl. We were raised in church. My family didn't attend but we were sent every time the Baptist bus pulled up at our house. I would stand on the side porch waiting for Mr. Dominic, the white pastor/bus driver/evangelist to come I remember standing on the porch in my white and green fluffy dress. The kind that had the bells in them so that every time I shook the bells would jingle. I'd shake

1976

it to the left and I'd shake it to her right. I'd shake a lot just to hear the bell ring.

When Mr. Dominic came to the house he'd personally get out of the bus, come to the porch and pick me up, lifting me higher than anyone else, and place me inside the bus. I loved that. He made me feel so special. He poured so much love into us. We all loved and adored Mr. Dominic.

My Grandmamma's faith was the weapon I would learn to use. It would be the help I'd cling to when life was hard. The melodies of her Bible stories would ring in my soul—showing me that hope was a prayer away. I didn't know then that what she showed me would give me the strength to overcome the things that lay ahead. My Grandmamma gave me my "fight".

There were many people who played a major role in my early years. Those who loved me instilled God and made an investment that would guide me later in life.

Up until this point things weren't so bad. Of course being locked in a closet was abusive, but certainly it was something I could handle. It would be something of little significance when compared to the abuse suffered later.

Bald Headed Charlie

That's what they called me

Piercing my identity

With words that hurt me...

All for a laugh

Or to feel higher than they should

Tearing me down letter by letter

Of destructive words that could

Words that crushed me

In-spite of myself

Words that mocked me

Made my hate myself...

I wish for an escape

From this world that flaunts

Running, Running, Running

Running from this place- the life that haunts

~ Chapter 3 ~

Bald Headed Charlie

This part is the most difficult to write. It was a part I would love to have left out. It's easier to mask my feelings about this issue. I still have pain in this area that has to be healed. My healing comes as I write for you. I've come face-to-face with my feelings of longing and desperation for love.

The longing began as a little girl born in a county hospital.

"Bald-Headed Charlie"

That was my childhood nickname.

My oldest sister was the one who ordained me with the name. She was three years older than me. She was the epitome of what every black girl wanted to look like. She had light colored skin and long hair.

Bald Headed Charlie

I despised the name "bald-headed Charlie. I despised my sister too. My sister and I didn't get along during our childhood. I was often the brunt of her jokes of too often found myself at the end of her punches. I felt second-class in comparison to her. She seemed to have everything going for her—even at a young age.

Her daddy came around to visit her and my brother.

I hated both the name bald-headed and the name Charlie. Those names would tell stories of my childhood: stories of lack, rejection, and sickness of my body and sickness of my soul

I heard it that name everyday. My cousins even started teasing me. My sister made fun of me about my hair or the lack thereof. She was a bright-skinned, longhaired, Daddy having girl. She made fun of me because I was bald headed, too black, ugly and didn't have a daddy. If I wasn't miserable about my life, she made sure I was.

She called me names all the time. But her main title for me was "Baldheaded Charlie." She called me this because I didn't have hair like everybody else and my Dad's name was supposed to be Charlie –at least from what my Grandmamma told me.

It was true, I was bald-headed, but through no fault of my own. I suffered with asthma and as a result, I was given a medication in which I still can't pronounce. The side of effect of this medication was hair loss. My hair came out a lot. I was so bald headed that I couldn't even comb my hair. All I could do was place a headband over the top of my head. Headbands were decoration for me though. I used them to let people know I was a girl. Bald-Headed Charlie.

That was me!

My mom was the youngest and only daughter out of four brothers. My uncles were married and had children. Everyone in my entire family had someone in their lives to call daddy - Everyone except me.

Bald Headed Charlie

I was the only one in the entire family who didn't have a relationship with a father. My sisters and brothers had their Dad, even if he didn't come around as often. They still had knowledge of who he was.

As far as my Dad, I had no idea where he was or even who he was. I longed to know him. I longed to feel the kisses of his mouth and experience his embrace. To know him would be to know me. My identity was connected to who he said I was. His silence communicated that I didn't exist.

I remember sitting in my Grandma's kitchen with my sister and her Dad. He had come over to visit her and my brother. He gave her a couple of dollars. A dollar was a lot back then, so a couple of dollars could buy a lot.

He reached to give me a dollar when she suddenly snatched it from his hand. She told me that he was her daddy and that I needed to get my own daddy. He took the dollar from her hand and gave it to me anyway.

She was right. He wasn't my daddy. He didn't have to give me a dollar. He didn't have to give me anything. He was a nice man, so he wasn't going to give her something in front of me—knowing that my feelings would be hurt.

My sister wanted her daddy all to herself and that included his money. I wondered how I was supposed to get my own daddy. I'm sure I had one somewhere. Every child had a daddy. It takes one to make a baby.

But I thought to myself and would've told her if I was brave enough that "I will get my own daddy and he's going to give me thousands of dollars and I'm not going to share, huh."

I knew that my Dad wasn't going to bring me thousands of dollars. He wasn't even going to bring me a dollar. If my dad hadn't shown up by now he was never coming.

I didn't know him and would never know what it felt like to jump into my daddy's lap and feel his loving embrace and protection. I struggled to know my existence, value, worth or purpose for being born. There was a huge hole in my soul and the name tattooed on it was "Daddy."

I spent countless days and hours envisioning him. I inspected each black man who passed by me wherever I was--hoping to get a little closer to the number one. I'd wonder "is that him?" or "is this him?"

I often wondered what he looked like.

Did I have his nose? Did I have his smile? Did I laugh like him? Every time I'd come up empty - never filling the void. What was it about me that made him reject me? Was I ugly? Was I bad? Was I a girl? Was I too dark? Whatever it was, it must've been pretty bad. It was more than obvious that he wanted nothing to do with me.

I couldn't understand why he didn't come see me. I was his seed. He created me. I didn't ask to be born. He could've stepped up to the plate. More than anything in the world he could've accepted me.

Oh, how I wanted to hear his voice. I wanted to hear him say, "Toya, I love you'" But the "I love you" never came and neither did he. Every part of me wished I was dead – I was anyway to him.

"If my Dad was to come"—I'd say to myself—"I'd let him know that I'm a "good girl". I made straight A's. I didn't get into trouble at school. Actually, the teacher said that I was smart. I would even sing for you daddy. I could sing for you daddy if you want me to. I'll clean the house daddy. I'll do whatever you want me to daddy—if you'll just come."

Still, he never came. Not on the weekends. Not on holidays. Not on my birthday. He never came in a phone call, birthday card or letter. He never came bearing gifts or carrying my favorite candy. I'd find myself sitting alone by the shade tree in the front yard wondering whom this man was that I wished to call daddy.

Who was this man? Why did he create me? How could he be so irresponsible to make a baby and then refuse to be part of her life? Can you imagine having a question that can never be answered? It eats at your soul. You feel as if life is mocking you. It knows something that you don't. Life knows you won't be protected. You are vulnerable and ashamed.

    My Mom refused to tell me my Dad's name or anything else about him for that matter. I don't know her reasons behind her refusal, but it didn't stop me from dreaming about him.

    Some days were harder than others. Every time I asked who my daddy was, I was constantly told I didn't need to know. So I just stopped asking. I wanted to know him and to know of his love for me. Every child needs to know that!

    My life would be incomplete without him. There were many times that I would become so engaged in the day-to-day childhood activity that I'd forget to think about him. I'd forget about all that pain until someone reminded me that he didn't want me. Every time they called out "bald-headed Charlie", I was reminded. The feelings of rejection and lack would flood my soul. All I wanted was to be accepted by everyone.

From one day to the next my feelings about him changed. One day I'd be angry, the next sad and the next one I'd love him. Day after day and year after year I felt this way.

I assumed that my Dad rejected me from conception. I figured he took the road of least resistance.

Out of sight--out of mind!

Staying out of sight would ensure that I was out of his mind. I hated the old adage "Momma's baby -Papa's maybe." I wished that "maybe" would've brought him to me. Then maybe I would've felt wanted, loved or even liked--just maybe.

My father's absence shadowed my life. It haunted me and I hated him. He didn't have to leave. He didn't have to leave me behind. I hated him for never trying to be a part of my life. I didn't ask to be born. I certainly didn't ask him to be my father. But he was – is.

It wasn't the medicine or the fact that I had asthma that tormented me. It wasn't the fact that my family members teased me about the condition over which I had no control. It was the pain of not having what made other girls beautiful: pretty light skin, long flowing hair and a family that loved her.

I was the ugly, bald-headed, black girl from 622 S.W. 15th street who didn't have a daddy. That's how everybody saw me and that's whom I saw. I was all of these things and more. I was "unloved".

Shortcomings made me different. I was-I am different!

Baldness represented the lack of life. Baldness represented rejection and the absence of covering from the man who conceived me. It demanded that I was not or ever would be good enough to have him in my life. It told me I was rejected and unloved.

It whispered that I could never be shaded from the heat of life. It had control and it viciously pursued me. My father, my mother, my creator gave it permission to burn me.

I was teased with the identity of a man I had never met.

Charlie!

The name reminds me of the old song: "Don't blame Mr. Charlie. Mr. Charlie is just a man."

Well, I did blame Mr. Charlie. Because Mr. Charlie was not just a man, he was supposed to be my father, daddy, pops or whatever we call them. I didn't care what his name was. I hated him and I loved him. I hated him because he didn't want me and I loved him because I wanted him.

My daddy chose to walk away from his responsibility. He never considered the impact his absence would have on my life. He had another life that commanded his attention. His life was more important than this little bald-headed girl in the big yellow house on the corner of 622 S.W. 15th street.

He left my mom to carry the burden of raising me alone. She had to foot the bill for milk, diapers and doctor's bills, which I'm sure was a lot of money since I was the hospital more than I was at home. Well, he left the bill to society because my Mom was on government assistance for as long as I can remember.

I was the result of my dad's own pleasure. I was his consequence--one he failed to face. Still, I hoped to one day see him face-to-face. I'd be able to ask him all the questions that I've ever thought. Why did he leave?

I thought to myself "I'd let him know that he didn't have to marry my mom, but he could've been an active part of my life."

I say "active" because he was a part of my life. He was part of my pain, disappointments and failures. His absence spoke louder than his presence. I couldn't change his choice.

The void I had in my heart would be filled with something. Life would fill it with despair, loneliness, fear and blindness.

There was no use in me getting my hopes up. I had hoped enough only to be let down. I did dream that one day I'd grow up and help little girls like me. I would be their rescuer. I'd tell them that they were smart and beautiful. I'd tell them that I loved them and that they were special. I wanted them to know that fairytales are for dreamers. If we wanted to be great in life, then we'd have to do it ourselves.

I hoped that one day I'd be able to tell them that.

Regardless of how strong I was determined to be, I was still a fragile little girl who wished for her daddy. Though I'd never admit it for fear of being talked about, I wanted to call anybody daddy. He didn't have to really be my daddy.

Isn't it ironic how names speak into your life? Bald headed Charlie is what they called me and baldheaded Charlie is what I answered to. The words that were spoken over me meant more than just critical songs rolling off the tongues of family members. I was a black bald headed girl with no daddy.

Every day I was reminded of this unfortunate fact. Bald-headed Charlie meant more than just a childhood nickname. Baldheaded Charlie

Bald Headed Charlie

meant that my daddy was gone-- just like the hair on the top of my sick little black head.

Sticks or Stones
Which should I choose?
If I could determine the outcome
Of my abuse...

Would it be the chants?
Or perhaps the knock upside my head
Would boast
Repeated blows of sticks and stones
Would destroy the most...

Perhaps, I should've ducked and dodged
The words from their mouths
Perhaps I should've stood taller
Should've shaken off their doubts...

Mistreated and abused
Teased and taunted
Bruised by the words
Rejected and haunted

Sticks and Stones

Didn't break my bones

But the words almost killed me

~ Chapter 4 ~

Sticks and Stones

"Sticks and stones may break my bones but words will never hurt me". I wish I knew who came up with that saying. I wonder what their world was like. The statement lies to us. Words have power.

They have the power to tear us down or to build us up. They tore me down - one word at a time.

Sticks and stones break didn't break my bones, but the hurtful words damaged my soul. I say to the person who created that statement that "sticks and stones did not break my bones but the words almost killed me".

I can't remember how many times I canted that saying as a young girl. I had no idea what it meant until I got older, but it sounded good. This phrase became my protection of sort. It sheltered me from the words that dripped from the lips of others.

Kids can be cruel and I know that from first-hand experience. Kids from school, on the neighborhood playgrounds and those who slept next to me at night were cruel. I don't think they meant to be, but people regurgitate what they know. I just got the brunt of the jokes.

Dark skin was taboo. If you've lived in America long enough, then you know the history of my people and how black skin was unacceptable. My skin has always been an issue in both the black and white cultures. I was too black for both of them.

Growing up was hard, but growing up black was an entirely different story.

From as early as I can remember, I felt like the black sheep of the family. In all honesty, I thought the black sheep was literally "a black sheep". I figured since my skin was dark, and black was not beautiful, a black sheep I'd be. I didn't realize the term meant more than just the color of skin.

To be the black sheep was to be the outcast - the different one. In many ways, I was the outcast, or at least I felt like the outcast and only God knew how different I would be.

Being a black sheep wasn't only about skin color—it was about different than everyone else. It was about feeling stupid, ugly, and black. I identified with the idea of being a black sheep. I identified with all these things and more.

Whatever hurtful words spoken over me regarding my skin tone or my intelligence, I ingested them.

My family was the first to tell me that my color was not beautiful, especially my oldest sister. She was a yellow hammer, which was a light-skinned black girl with skin that looked like a tanned white girl. . It was better to be a "yellow hammer" that the skin toned looked like a tanned white-girl.

Being lighter skinned was a treasure for my sister and other light-skinned girls like her. Beauty wasn't seen in dark skin and it certainly wasn't seen in me.

From yellow bone, paper bag, caramel and chocolate, we recognized by color and it made a difference.

It certainly made a difference for me. I was the outcast in both cultures. I was Black both in culture and skin tone. The closer you were to looking white the better you were and the likelihood of being accepted was greater.

My sister told me I had a white girl's lips, booty and that I even talked like a white girl. Every time I looked in the mirror I saw two people. I wasn't black enough physically for blacks and yet I was too black for them—my nose was too big and my skin too dark.

I was made fun of because my speech was "too proper". I spent a lot of time reading so I could be smart. I admired Martin Luther King, Jr. and desired to be like him. He was my hero. I admired his strength and determination. I dreamt of making a difference in the world just like he did.

I wasn't trying to be white by speaking well. I wanted to be educated.

I was left feeling confused about my place in the world. People talked about me because I had white girl features and they talked about me because I had features of a slave. I didn't know where to fit it or if I even did.

I don't blame my sister for anything. She was just as caught up in the racist world as I was. We all thought that beauty came in lighter skin tones. We were fed the lie through television, especially music videos, where every girl on the set was light-skinned with long, flowing hair, albeit real or fake.

I didn't despise my sister, but she found an opportunity as most kids do to tease their siblings and she pounced. She made sure that I never forgot the fact that I was black. How does a little girl fit in when she's the outcast? Who's the enemy--my skin or me?

The kids in my neighborhood called me African-Booty-Scratcher, which meant that I was from Africa and scratched my booty. It was definitely not a compliment. On top of being called names by the black kids, the white kids at school called me "nigger". I couldn't make it anywhere. I spent a lot of time defending myself from those darts.

I aimed to extinguish the fiery darts of the hurtful words. The words were spoken to destroy myself esteem--if I had any to destroy. The fact that I had breath in my body made me a target for everyone who came across my path.

I couldn't fight back with my black pride, so I clung to education. I was determined to win somehow and if education worked for Martin Luther King, then it would work for me.

My soul was thirsting for acceptance. I needed somebody at some point to look beyond my physical appearance and love the little girl that was on the inside. I knew that I had to keep fighting no matter how tough it got.

My soul was dried out at this point. I was screaming, "here I am—see me". I wanted those in my life to see and appreciate me for who I was. I wanted them to see that I was human and had feelings just like them. All the wanting and desiring in the world didn't change anything. I was still me and they still hated me.

My friends and I chanted phrases like "the blacker the berry—the sweeter the juice" or "black is beautiful, black is sweet, black is something you shole can't be". We'd make sure we had a lot of attitude when we said it—concluding each phrase with our hands on our hips, moving our arms in a circle motion and snapping our fingers.

I don't know who invented those phrases, but they worked for us. I can't speak for my friends, but I used them to protect me against the comments that tore me down. It became easier and easier to get an attitude than it was to keep taking everything that was dished out.

This was my way of fighting back. I couldn't change the fact that I was black. God made me. I don't know why God made me black. I long ago stopped trying to figure out why God did things. Maybe He needed somebody to laugh at.

I wanted pretty, silky, white skin. I wanted to be beautiful just like the light-skinned girls in the videos who put tons of weave in their hair so that they could look white. I wanted to be white but I wanted to stand up and declare that "black is beautiful".

When things got too hard for me, I'd find a quiet spot outside to cry and pray. I liked talking to God—if he existed.

I'd sit and talk about my dreams and how it felt like the whole world was against me. I'd tell him I was going to be great one day. I wasn't going to let anyone keep me down.

I was always a little stronger after these little quiet moments. It was a nice retreat from the hurting world that I endured everyday.

Things didn't change much around me, but I was stronger after my visits with God. I had more fight in me.

If my people could fight racism with education, then I could beat the world too.

The more they taunted—then the more I'd read. Reading was my way out. By reading I could escape this hateful world and be anybody that I wanted to be. I could go to any place in the world and be free. I could be what everyone said I couldn't be and that was being me.

I'm satisfied that every kid had something to say was hurting in their own world. They were pouring onto me what had been poured into them. It's human nature to pass on what has been learned. I drank their words into my fiber.

I embellished each drop. Each drink burned, but I kept drinking. It was the only source of water that I had. It was hurtful but it would do for a while. At least I was being noticed.

The teasing however didn't stop with the kids. The adults had something to say as well. The words from adults meant more to me than what the kids in the neighborhood or at school had to say. Those kids didn't know anything. They were just kids. I definitely figured that adults would only speak those things that are true. Surely they know more about life than any kid I knew.

When I was about ten, I got up one Sunday morning got dressed in the best clothes that I could find and walked five blocks to the one of many churches in the neighborhood.

I put on a small blue dress decorated with little, yellow flowers with white, lace ruffles that were pleated on the front. I found a pair of white stockings with a hole in the leg. A hole in a pair of stockings wasn't a big deal. I didn't want to be late for church, so I put them on and out the door I went.

When I got to the church I walked in and about five minutes later I walked out.

Two women who were sitting in the back saw me come in and started talking about the clothes that I was wearing. They laughed amongst themselves about the holes in my stockings and the too little dress that I had on.

Two grown women, who should've been examples of love and acceptance, since they were in the Lord's house, treated me just like everybody else had done.

I walked out of the church that day in tears. The walk back home was slow. I walked every five blocks back home with tear-filled eyes. The tears rolled down my face just like they had done many times before. Each tear found its familiar trail down my cheeks hitting the hot pavement. The hole in my stocking seemed to be much bigger than it did when I put them on that morning.

One of my uncles was a truck driver. He was on the road for weeks at a time, so any chance I had to see him was appreciated. Each time he'd pull up in his 18-wheeler, I'd run and jump into him arms. He'd pick me up and squeeze me until I could barely breathe. My legs would dangle under me the more he squeezed.

Borrowed Water

He'd squeeze me so hard my legs would go numb. He made sure that he always brought some type of snack every time he came. He knew that my favorite candy was Skittles. If he didn't bring me a bag, then he would give me a dollar or two so that I could buy whatever I wanted.

Then something changed in my Uncle. He changed towards me. I don't know why. As I got older—he grew colder.

He took advantage of every opportunity to put me down he could get. He and my mom would tell me "I had all the book sense in the world but no common sense." I'd think long and hard about what they said but still couldn't figure it out. I'd picture a cent sign and wonder what that had to do with me.

My uncle was very good at confusing us kids. He'd ask us to do something for him in a riddle. We had to figure out what he was saying before we could do what he wanted. We'd get stumped every time. It wasn't out of fun and games that he did this, nor was he trying to sharpen our thinking skills.

When I couldn't figure out what he was asking he'd spew off comments like "girl you're as dumb as a box of rocks." Again, I had no idea what he meant, so I'd try to picture a literal box of rocks—wondering how I could be compared to that. I just didn't understand.

I was about eleven when I realized what they were saying to me. They were telling me I was stupid. A box of rocks does nothing. It can't speak, think or move. If I was dumber than that, then I was pretty dumb. I thought I was smart. I made straight A's in school. My third grade teacher, Mrs. Haney, always told me how smart I was. I was smarter than my entire class.

I couldn't figure out why my Uncle went to such great lengths to make me feel low. I didn't understand why he wanted to put me down. I thought that he would've or at least should've been proud of me for getting an education, especially since he only went as far as the seventh grade.

I couldn't figure out the riddle to give him what he wanted. Not figuring it out meant I was going to get a whooping. Yes, I got a whooping for not figuring out what he was asking. He enjoyed taking off his thick leather belt, the kind with the name of the owner sewn on it. He'd whip it off in one swoop and would commence to beat me. If I was going to avoid being beaten then I knew that I had to get better at figuring out his riddles.

One day my cousin, brother and I were sitting at the kitchen table eating a can of hominy because there was nothing else to eat. The only thing in the refrigerator to eat was dead roaches and a bottle of mustard. We were eating the very last can of food in the house and we were eating it cold.

While we were eating, my Uncle came into the house with several bags of food. He had cookies, bread, lunchmeat, cheese, potato chips and a gallon of juice. Every bone in my body leaped for joy. We were so hungry. He was our salvation.

He sat the food out on the table and told us that we could eat whatever we wanted. He told us it didn't matter to him how much we ate—we could eat it all.

Unfortunately for me, my eyes were bigger than my stomach. I piled my plate with two sandwiches several cookies, as many chips as my hands could hold and a big cup of juice. It didn't take much food to fill my stomachs. After a few bites I was full. I couldn't eat all the food I had put on my plate.

Because I didn't eat all the food, he pulled off his leather belt and whooped me. He told me that I was being too greedy and shouldn't have put all that food on my plate. This treatment left me confused and intimidated. He bullied me into a position where he had control and the end result was a whooping.

I couldn't win for losing.

My Uncle set me up to fail. He knew that I wasn't going to be able to eat all the food.

He tricked me. He came into the house with the intent on tricking us as he had done before.

I hated him that day and I hated bologna sandwiches, vanilla cookies, Lay's potato chips and orange drink. I hated eating and I hated living.

No matter how hard I tried I always came to the same conclusion—nobody cared. In my eyes no one cared and knew from that point on I could trust no one. I was cautious of everybody around me. I felt like everybody had an agenda and it included abusing me.

Regardless of what happened I was still going to be better. They were not going to hold me back. I told myself to work harder because they were a bunch of ignorant people who were jealous of me.

Even though I attempted to fight back with my determination, I still believed what they told me. I was still a slave to their thoughts of me, their words against me and their lack of love for me.

From that day on I looked upon my Uncle with hatred in my heart. I was disgusted with his tactics and I was disgusted with him. He was fat and uneducated and I promised myself that I would never be like him.

The Uncle I once loved and adored-- I now hated and despised.

My opinion of him didn't change until I became an adult and realized that people do what they know. I won't go far as to say that they didn't know any better. I wouldn't justify abusive behavior. He knew better and my Mom certainly knew better.

Or did they?

They were feeding me the same water they had been fed. While that could be an excuse—there has to come a point in a person's life when they decide to act better than what they were taught. I guess it was easier for them to stay in the condition that they were in and to put me down to make themselves feel better—smarter.

Sticks and Stones create wounds that can heal in a matter of days or weeks, but Words can have a lifetime affect. Imagine the damage done to a bleeding heart and soul. Hurtful words sink deep into the silent places.

They hide in the crevices of the wounded. They link themselves with the abandoned, rejected, and lonely. They take residence. They take control. They whisper in your ear each time you step out to take on a new challenge. They jingle in your sleep. Every opportunity for a better life is confronted with these words. They remind you of who you are and they put you in your place--"Don't go thinking more than you ought, now" they declare.

The wounds from sticks and stones can be seen; therefore, they can be nursed back to health. I could fix the damage. However, the wounds left by the words of those in my life couldn't be seen nor could they be healed. Whether the words were bald-headed Charlie, African-Booty-Scratcher, nigger or being told that I was dumb as a box of rocks or that I had no common sense—they all had the same affect.

Sticks and Stones

No 'Word' was less powerful than the other. The words left deep wounds on my self-esteem and self-worth. These wounds festered and slowly infected every part of my life. Every decision that I would make was first dictated by what I heard.

Sticks and Stones, huh? If I had a choice—I'd choose these any day.

Now I lay me down to sleep
I pray the Lord my body to keep
If I should be molested

Before I wake
I pray the Lord
My soul to take...

Don't let him touch me through the night
Protect my innocence
Protect my rights
Please send an angel
Strong and mighty
With a sword of fire
To protect me...

He's now violated my dreams
Awakened his passion out of my sleep
Satisfying lust that drips from his fangs
Now I Lay Me Down to weep...

~ Chapter 5 ~

Now I Lay Me Down To Weep

Since the age of five, every man who came into my life abused me in one-way or another. Whether it was molestation, rape or consensual sex for their own gratification, my body was target practice for the lustful desires of perverted men.

The gates of hell welcomed my life. This plan was to destroy me. Even though I was taught about God from an early age, the pain from abuse blotted God out. I couldn't see the protection he showed my Grandmamma time and time again. He never sent an angel to help me, especially on the night that changed my life forever.

The abuse that you'll read about crippled me since the age of eight. It consumed me and it controlled my life. I suffered with low self-esteem for years because of the lessons learned from the night my body, innocence and childhood was taken from me.

I don't remember exactly when he came into my room; he was my Mom's boyfriend and the father of four of my siblings. I didn't even hear when he approached the pallet on the floor where I was sleeping. I remember my mom's boyfriend waking me up, telling me to go into the back bathroom. I was very sleepy but I did what I was told. The house was pitch-black.

I stumbled through each room bumping into dressers, doors and shoes that had been left on the floor. I couldn't distinguish my hand from his faint silhouette in front of me. I made sure to stay as close to him as possible.

When we got to the bathroom he stepped inside first and turned on the light. I stepped in behind him and he closed the door. He told me to lie down on the floor.

So I did.

I lay down in front of the toilet seat with my head touching the bathtub. He got down on his knees and pushed my nightgown up over my waist. He took off my panties and with no warning he put his largest finger inside me. I was no longer sleepy. "Ouch"

"Shut up before somebody hears you," he forcefully whispered.

I wished for someone to hear me. I didn't understand what was happening, but I didn't like it. It was hurting me. I didn't feel good. I started to cry. Each teardrop ran down my face and hit my chest like bullets. He was killing me. He was destroying every essence of my femininity. He was destroying my future and my childhood all in one moment.

He twirled his finger inside of me for his pleasure and my pain. I tried to pull my body away but it didn't work. He had his mind set on molesting me. He was enjoying himself. I lay my head back against the tub wishing that I were somewhere else—wishing that I was somebody else. I hated me. I hated him liking me. I hated being touched. I hated being.

I silently cried out to the God my Grandmother knew-- the God who sent an angel to watch over us when we were alone. I cried for him to send me the angel. "God help me!" "He's stronger than me—I can't fight him!" "Am I supposed to fight him?" "Don't you protect little girls?"

"Oh, God make him stop." "Godddd" I silently cried.

Pain was reeling from my little eight-year old pure body. He attempted to insert another finger when I screamed again. Fortunately, he told me to forget it because I was making too much noise. He treated me as if I was his mistress. I didn't ask him to introduce me to the world of perversion. I didn't ask him to put his dirty fingers inside me.

Now I Lay Me Down to Weep

I certainly didn't ask him to get pleasure from my innocent body.

I was instructed to go back to bed. I got up from the floor feeling sick and dizzy. My vagina was throbbing with pain. It felt swollen. I quietly made my way back to the pallet trying not to wake anyone. My cries had turned into sniffles. I didn't want anyone to hear my shame that I now carried.

When I got to the pallet, I flopped my abused body down—hoped that everything had been a dream. I knew it wasn't. The pain was too real. There were no childhood dreams that night. There weren't any fairytales to be relished.

I was no longer a little girl. This man just forced me into the world of twisted womanhood.

The next morning was like any other day. Our daily routine was for all the kids to get up by seven o'clock, eat breakfast and go outside to play. Several of my siblings and I were standing in my Granddaddy's room getting ready to go outside when he came into the room. He handed me a dollar and told me to not to tell anybody what happened.

I knew he'd done something wrong and was trying to pay me off. He treated me like a prostitute. He got his pleasure, now he was trying to pimp me with a dollar. Only a crumbled up one dollar bill. That was my value—one dollar.

I took the dollar, as any kid would've, and I bounced my way to the candy lady's house and bought myself a nice stash of one-cent candy. I bought 100 pieces of candy. It wasn't as good as the candy my granddaddy gave me, but it was sweet and it took away the pain.

Even though the abuse was bitter, I at least felt wanted. For some time I felt appreciated. For once I was accepted even if the acceptance came at such a heavy price. I held a twisted view of love and acceptance—a twisted view that lead me down a treacherous path of continuous pain and agony.

Finally somebody noticed me. Even the bitter tasted sweet. I learned two things that day. I learned that when a man wants your body, then you give it to him. I learned that I had no value. I was reduced to a one-dollar bill

    This man's lust sought and conquered me. I figured that he must've watched me all day; enjoying the way I walked; enjoying the way I played with my siblings or even watched how I might've plopped my legs open while I was sitting on the floor. He must've strategized the perfect time to rip my destiny to shreds—destroying my innocence.

    Fortunately, that was the last time he would ever touch me, but the damage had been done. It would take the rest of my life, even to this date, to overcome that tragedy. He took my childhood away from me. That single perverted act changed my whole world. He awakened the woman inside of me and now I was the one on the prowl.

    Hell hath no fury like a black, bald-headed, girl molested.

    Many called me "fast" or "hot-to-trot" because of the change in my behavior. I liked it when the boys at school touched my butt and told me that I was fine. I was enamored with male body parts and I liked the feel of them in my hand. I enjoyed seeing it and touching it.

I started playing sex games with boys in the neighborhood. "Hide and go get it" was my favorite game. It was played like hide-n-go-seek, but when the person was caught, they had to do something sexual to the other person.

I would have my neighbor take off his pants and lie under a pile of leaves and pretend that he was a monster. I would lay on the ground pretending to be a damsel in distress. My friend would jump from the leaves and lay on top of me. We didn't know how to have sex then, but we knew how to "goose," or have pretend sex with clothes on.

I even played games with my cousins. We didn't have sex, but I tried to have sex with them. I tried every time I got that throbbing sensation. It was a reminder to me that I was a woman. The pulsating urge was my indicator that I needed something inside me.

A short time after all of this, for no known reason, I was sent to live with my Uncle Berry who lived at the end of the street.

My uncle had three boys. That was a bad move on my Mom's part, but she didn't know. One day my cousin and I were sent to take a nap. We weren't sleepy so we just started playing. That familiar urge hit me like a ton of bricks. One thing led to another and before I knew it I had taken off my panties and grabbed his penis and brought him closer to me when my oldest cousin walked into the room.

I was busted.

Needless to say I was sent back home. I never heard any discussions about what I had done, but when I walked into my Grandmamma's house I saw shame on everyone's face. My mom looked at me like she was disgusted. It was at that moment I knew what "shame" felt like. I felt like the nastiest, dirtiest girl in the world.

The abuse sent me into a whirlwind of insecurity, fear and false belief that having sex with someone would be my only means of gaining acceptance. Perverse, sexual affection was better than no affection at all. I decided to accept whatever form of love and acceptance that came my direction. It didn't matter who or what the source was. I just wanted love and if I had to be abused to get it—then so be it.

I endured pain, rejection and abuse time and time again—searching for the pure love that never came. For some reason that was fine with me. Abuse, after all, is all I knew.

I figured that the sum of my life would be failure. The failure to make people love me, accept me and enjoy me. I had a lot to offer, but I couldn't get anyone else to see it. I placed this thinking on my back and carried it with me throughout my life.

My mom broke up with the molester for whatever reason. I was more than glad. She went from that relationship into another one immediately. I was afraid this boyfriend would have his way with me as well. I wanted to make sure he became so afraid of me that he wouldn't even consider molesting me. Since no one else was going to protect me, then I had to protect myself.

My motive was to make sure he didn't come near me. I was going to give him hell and I did. I made sure that he hated me. I always had an attitude and I always talked back. I refused to do anything he asked. I talked about him.

I'd rather him hate me than like me and find him creeping into my room late at night.

People talked about my behavior, but they didn't know what had happened. They said that I was "fass" and was "always up in boys faces."

They couldn't look beyond my behavior and see the abuse because they didn't know it occurred. Instead of questioning my behavior they chose to ridicule me because of it.

I wished they would've understood my behavior. But they didn't. I was more than a "fass" little girl who liked boys too much. I was a hurting kid who wanted to be noticed.

Little did I know that the abuse I suffered would haunt me for many, many years. It would be the cornerstone of the building in my life. It tainted my life song. I was too young to understand how deeply my life was affected. For years I carried and I blamed myself for what had happened.

It ruined me in ways that I was too young to understand.

He took away my childhood. He molested my hopes and dreams.

There were times as an adult when I wanted to be raped. I wanted to be taken advantage of because that was all I knew. I didn't want to give my permission for a man to have sex with me. If he raped me then I couldn't be blamed.

Every time a man approached me for sex I'd feel like that eight-year old again--alone and overpowered. These men didn't approach me in a threatening manner but that didn't matter. My thinking was already locked up. I was bound by the lie that I had to give a man what he wanted.

I know that this was a very sick way of thinking, but that's how I felt. I didn't think that I had the right to tell a man that he couldn't have me.

I didn't understand that my body belonged to me and that I did have the right to tell a man no. I didn't enjoy sex for the most part. It was mechanical. It was robotic.

I'd think that maybe the sex would be good enough to make this man or that man like me. That never happened. While I did become engaged in several relationships, they were still founded on sex. That's all we did. We didn't talk, go to the movies or out to eat—we just had sex. It meant nothing and neither did I.

I was searching and searching for someone to love me. Being stuck in this whirlwind of destruction was tormenting. I wanted to change my behavior, but I didn't know what to change or how to change it. I wasn't sure I'd be better off if I did change. I feared everything that lay ahead. It was unknown and I'd rather stay where I was—even though it hurt—than to walk down a road that might prove worse.

Have you ever seen a hamster spin on a wheel? They find entertainment in the wheel going round and round. My life was that of a hamster. I was going round and round and ending up nowhere. I was doing the same things over and over again—finding myself more hurt and disappointed than before.

The pain crippled me. It taught me to mask my feelings and become hard. Hard people can't feel; therefore, hard people can't hurt. I would pretend--as I did that day in my Granddaddy's room when Jay gave me that dollar—that nothing had happened. I would walk through life and make everyone think I was fine. I would protect myself from the world.

What I didn't understand is that my mask hindered me from feeling all emotions good and bad. A part of me didn't care anyway. I was tired of trying to feel. Feelings were for the weak. I would be strong. My strength turned into death. I died on the inside.

The abuse cost me healthy relationships with men. I lost my attraction for men. I didn't want to be touched, looked at or wanted in a loving way. I was afraid of touch. Abuse always seemed to follow touch. Men always abused me anyway.

I built some very tall walls around my life. All my walls hid the pain of rejection, abuse, neglect and turmoil. I was comfortable with my walls though. I learned to live life with their existence.

The abuse not only perverted my relationship with men, it twisted my relationship with people. I was so mad at the world that I had a hard time determining the people who genuinely wanted to love me.

One day I looked around at my walls and saw for the first time that they represented the closet I was placed in as a little girl. I hadn't come very far from the long ago torture I had endured. I had placed myself in an emotional closet—hidden from the rest of the world.

Every part of me wanted to remain hidden, but every part of me wanted to let the world know I was here to stay. I decided not to let that man molest me my entire life. Every time I ran from people or built another wall I was giving him power to control my life.

For years I lived my life in the shadows of my abuser. I blamed myself for the abuse. I was mad at the world. I wished for death. I continuously contemplated killing myself—as a kid and as an adult. My self-esteem wasn't just low—it didn't exist.

I had every right to feel what I felt. I did nothing wrong. It wasn't my fault and I began to rest in that fact. I believed I could be brave enough to walk into my healing and never have to carry the shame placed on me.

Such is strange land
Don't know where to go
The path that follows
Me
Refuse to direct or show
Left alone
To care for me
All alone
Was ordained to be
Noodles in the day
Nothing at night
Fighting hunger pains
Despair lingered in sight
Keep moving
Keep forging ahead
Hope is on the horizon
But desperation is not dead
War of two worlds
Fighting for my soul
Vulnerable to sadness
Left on my own

~ Chapter 6 ~

On My Own

Eventually, we all moved out of my Grandmother's house because the water didn't work and neither did the electricity. My Mom was given a voucher by the city to find another place to live. Everyone left, including my Grandma—she went to live with one of my uncles. The house was left completely empty.

We moved into a one-bedroom apartment across town. Eight of us lived in the apartment--my six siblings, my Mom and me. We had to sleep anywhere we could. Well, we had two options—the couch or the floor. It was a living arrangement I had become accustomed.

On My Own

The apartment we moved into was directly upstairs from the man who molested me. I stayed as far away from him and my apartment. I started hanging out with kids who smoked weed, drank beer and had sex. I wasn't immediately influenced by their behavior, but it was fun to hang out with them.

I met a boy who later became the father of my son. I really didn't like him but he was nice and cool to hang out with. He was 17 and I was 12. I never really thought about having sex with him. He was just a friend who thought I was cute. We hung out everyday but I still had no attraction to him.

We also had a neighbor who lived next door named Rita. Rita was a nice lady but she was also a drug addict. She smoked crack cocaine. Even though she was a dope fiend, Rita took good care of her son. I liked Rita a lot. She was nice to me. I liked her because she was feisty.

She didn't take mess from anybody. She reminded me of the 1970's Cleopatra Jones.

Rita was also very pretty. It was sad that she had let the drugs get the best of her. She didn't look like a dope fiend. She kept herself up and her house clean. She always wore make-up. A lot of men came to Rita's house. Some came to use her house for smoking crack and some came to hit on her.

My mom moved to Dallas with her new boyfriend shortly after we moved into the apartment. He had a one-bedroom apartment as well. There was no way that all seven of us and my mom could live with him.

I definitely didn't want to live in close quarters with a man I didn't know or trust. I didn't like Dallas either. So, my mom let us live wherever we wanted to. We were scattered--all living in different homes. She moved to Dallas by herself. I ended up moving in with Rita.

Rita's money was limited. She didn't work and she smoked crack. She got her money from her monthly AFDC check. We didn't have food to eat most of the time. I'd go to school and borrow money from my friends—fifty cents here and there. When I got home I'd go the store and buy packages of Ramen noodles.

At the time, they were ten cents a package.

If I had fifty cents then I could eat on noodles for five days. I'd use the rest of the money—if I were fortunate to get more—to buy hair and feminine products. My hair was 'nappy' and the kids at school let me know just how nappy it was. They talked about me a lot--my clothes never fit right or I wore the same ones over and over again—it was always something.

I didn't have very many friends at school, especially black friends. Either they were intimidating because they always seemed to want to fight or I was timid because I was in unfamiliar territory. Either way, we didn't bond. That's how I lived.

I could've quit school, but I didn't want to live my life the way others lived theirs. I was left on my own, left to fend for myself. No one was going to protect me. I had to learn to protect myself if I was going to survive.

Education had always been important to me. It was important enough to my ancestors that many of them died to have it and to pass it on. I knew that education was power. It caused men to become great.

It enabled those who beheld its glory to overcome obstacles and achieve things slaves dreamed about. I wanted to be counted in the number of greatness. I was going to make my ancestors proud.

For those reasons I was determined to stay in school. I wanted more from life. I needed my life to be more than what I saw around me--more than a child molester and more than a drug addict. I didn't want to end up like my mom either. I didn't want to be stuck with seven kids with no one around to help raise them. I despised the people around me and they weren't educated. At least if I learned all I could, then I was more likely not to end up like them. Education meant freedom.

On My Own

Living with Rita wasn't bad but it was dangerous. There were times when I would wake up in the middle of the night and see the house full of men hitting the crack pipe. I watched as they started "geeking" after each hit. They'd get paranoid—thinking someone was after them. One man got up, ran to the window and started peeping out. He thought the police were outside. He'd open part of the curtain just enough to peep outside and then he'd shut it and stand with his back against the wall—hoping the police who were supposed to be outside--didn't see him.

I watched this dog and pony show for a while and then went back to bed. That was my life with Rita. I watched events like this many times during my stay with her. I was in a vulnerable environment. I could've been hurt, raped or even killed. However, no one ever touched me. Even a dope fiend had enough sense to know that you don't molest little girls I felt safe at her house.

Rita was upset that my mom left me with her with no support. She'd give me her spiel of what she thought about my Mom. She called her "sorry and no good." At that time I agreed.

    Rita told me I wouldn't have to listen to my Mom if I were to get pregnant. She told me that my Mom couldn't tell me what to do if I had my own baby. I could even go down to the welfare office and get food stamps and an AFDC check to support my baby and me. It sounded like a plan to me. It was right up my alley. Rebellion was setting in. I was determined to be in control of my life.

    I eventually started having sex with Labron. Even though I didn't like him, my goal was to use him to get what I wanted—my freedom. He was the weapon to get away from my Mom's control. I no longer wanted to live with her or abide by her rules because I didn't respect her.

    I was mad at her for not taking better care of us. I was mad at her for putting me in the closet and beating me every time she felt like it. I was mad at her for putting me in a position to be molested. I was mad at her for leaving me to live with a drug addict. I was mad at her for not coming to see if I needed food, water or to check and see if I was even alive.

In my opinion she was the last person that I'd run to for help. I never felt safe with her. I felt that since I was already living on my own then she didn't have the right to tell me anything. I just needed to seal the deal.

Labron and I had sex everywhere we could: in the alley, at his house, at his friend's house. I went so far as to break into my molester's apartment and have sex on his bed. I didn't enjoy what I was doing, but I was no longer in control.

Most of the time I zoned out—letting him have his way with me. I would subconsciously go numb so I wouldn't feel him and most of the time my mind was absent. I'd go to another place. A place where there was no feeling and no pain--a place hidden from the rest of the world--my own secret place. I could be whatever I wanted to be— do whatever I wanted to do. This place of bliss only existed in my mind but kept me sane. I couldn't escape the pain that my present world was bringing me, but I could escape in my mind.

It always seemed like no matter how hard I tried to overcome the hurdles in my life, there would always be a surprise around the corner. Right when I thought that things would turn around there was another tragedy to remind me of my place in this world. Just when I was at the point of trusting—people would fail me again.

One day I was on the school bus coming home from school. The bus arrived at the bus stop. Before it stopped I saw two friends of mine standing at the stop. I thought it was strange that they were standing on the corner, but I didn't put much thought into it. Maybe they were just chilling. The bus came to stop and I got off.

As soon as the bus left one of the girls walked up to me and punched me in the face. The other one jumped in. I was being jumped in broad daylight. I was being attacked for no reason. I had done nothing wrong to them. I'm sure they had something better to do than plot all day to jump me. There was no need in me trying to fight back.

Blood was flying everywhere. My blood was flying everywhere. I was scared and puzzled. Why were they beating me up? I didn't do anything to them.

I never had that question answered. I guess they wanted someone to beat up and that someone was me.

I was left a bloody mess. I didn't try to fight back. I was too afraid to fight in fear of what would happen if I did. I was thankful that my nose wasn't broken or my face permanently scarred.

After they beat me up, they took off running toward their house. I was thankful to for the relief. I didn't know how much more I could've endured.

I picked myself up from the ground where I had been pummeled. I looked around to see if anyone had seen them, but there wasn't a soul in sight. Dazed and confused I stumbled my way home past the barking dogs and vacant homes. What in the heck just happened? I don't know what caused them to jump me. I don't know why they plotted this attack all day. How did I become a target again?

Everything I had ever felt about life was confirmed. People can't be trusted no matter how young or old they are. I believed that people were out to get me. I couldn't do anything right. Besides it wouldn't have mattered. The familiar theme of rejection and abuse that had run through my life boasted its presence in my heart. I felt like America's most unwanted. Abuse came from all directions.

When was I going to learn that I couldn't hide from the fierce grip of destruction? I should've known they weren't going to like me—no one had ever liked me before so what made me think that they were going to start now that I was on my own. I believed in giving people a chance but that chance seemed to continuously turn out to be pain.

That's how the world operates--always planning sneak attacks. Either I would learn to divert these attacks or I would succumb each time. By this time I was a very angry little girl. I was mad at everybody. I was mad at God. I was mad at Mom, I was mad at those stupid girls, I was mad at the molester and I was mad at the people who were supposed to protect me. If they would've done their jobs then I wouldn't be getting beat up every time I turned around.

    I needed a change in my life, but I couldn't do anything about it. I was only twelve. I was tired of being isolated from a normal life. Was it too much just to ask for some peace? At the age of eleven I had been abandoned by my mom, lived with a dope fiend, hustled money to feed myself, endured abuse with each human interaction. I was tired. Life had dealt me a bad hand and I was too young to play the game.

    I lived with Rita for several more months before my Mom came and got me. She came a few weeks too late. I was already pregnant. We moved in with her boyfriend's sister, Sharon, in a two-bedroom apartment. In a very short time they picked on the pregnancy. Sharon frequently told my Mom that I was pregnant because I was sleeping too much. I was so glad she told her. I wanted her to know so she could leave me alone for good.

Early one morning I overheard Sharon and my Mom discussing the homemade abortion I was going to have. They were debating whether or not I could be pregnant. Sharon suggested to my Mom that she give me ginger tea, which would make me have a miscarriage.

They were trying to abort my baby. I had lived in the streets long enough to know how to get over. I wasn't going to let them take away the only person in the world that would eventually love me. They were crazy. They didn't care about me anyway. I wouldn't have been pregnant if she hadn't left me to take care of myself. Sure she left me with an adult—but come on—a dope fiend.

I had lived on my own for several months. She left me in an adult world. I stepped into those adult shoes and ended up doing what adults do. I thought I was grown and nobody could tell me anything. I didn't want to be rebellious, but I was angry and I was hurting.

When my Mom gave me the tea she told me to drink all of it. I took a small sip to make her think I was going to drink the whole cup but when she turned her back I poured the tea in a towel that was sitting on the cabinet. She had no clue what I had done. She assumed I drank the tea and that it just didn't work.

Our stay with Sharon was short. My Mom received another housing voucher and we moved back to Grand Prairie. I enrolled in Lee Middle School as a 12 year-old pregnant student. All eyes were on me. I don't remember hearing any comments, but I'm sure they were being made.

Things between my Mom and I got worse. I ran away several times during this period. I hung out with the wrong crowd but didn't engage in any of their drugs activities. Living with Rita showed me the dim realities of a life on drugs. I saw hot smoking weed turned to smoking crack. I saw what it did to Rita. It stole her life and I didn't ever want to live like she did. I needed to stay away from drugs if I was ever going to make it.

When I was eight months pregnant I was hanging out with some friends at the Key Motel. The Key Motel is where a lot of teens hung out and had sex. Two teenage girls rented a room so everybody could have sex without the fear of getting caught. They allowed everybody to come in and have sex. There was a lot of sex happening in that room too. I thought it was nasty though, so I didn't participate. I couldn't imagine the filth and disease that was on those beds.
However, it was at the Key Motel that I met Richard. He had smooth black skin and a thug look. I didn't know much about him but I wanted him. We wouldn't hook up until later, but he was on my mind constantly.

My son's father had cheated on me with one his neighbors and needless to say, he moved on. That is what usually happens when a young girl gets pregnant. The guy all of a sudden has an epiphany that you're not the one he wants.

If he was going to move on, then so was I. I had my son in August and by September my older sister, who also had two children by this time, and I moved into our own apartment. It wasn't a wise decision on the part of the adults in our lives. My sister was only 16 and I was 13. We had people in our apartment all day, every day. Our house was full of teenagers on a daily basis.

Of course, we were all having sex. Out of everyone that came over, I was the only one who didn't drink or smoke. I wanted to be in complete control of my surroundings. I couldn't afford to be taken advantage of again. There were fights and orgies almost every weekend. It was chaos, but I was used to chaos. I could live with twenty people in the house. If I could sleep in a house with a bunch of "geeked-out" dope fiends, then I could sleep anywhere.

I tried to create order a lot. I'd have to kick people out only to have my sister allow them back in. I was the only teenager who went to school everyday. They laughed at me—called me nerd and party pooper. They had no clue that I was just tired. I needed peace some time. I went to school everyday because I was determined not to be like them. I wanted more out of life and education was my ticket out of the mess.

Things changed and they changed quickly. I found myself pregnant again--two kid and two different daddies. I was pregnant by Richard—you know the dark-skinned thug from the motel. I couldn't be surprised. I was having sex with him. Another baby wasn't part of my plan. The first pregnancy was my way to get out from under my Mom's control but this time it was different. I didn't want any more kids. There was nothing that I could do about it though.

I wasn't having sex to make babies. I was searching for love. Love is what I wanted but a baby is what I got.

I'm sure you can guess that he too disappeared. I heard the age-old "it's not my baby" song that most teen mothers hear. He didn't come around the house that much anymore. But his friends did. He had one friend in particular named Crazo. Crazo was cool most of the time, but there would be times when he would do something off the wall in order to live up to his name.

One evening a couple of friends and I were in my room listening to music. I was talking on the phone with a friend. Crazo came into the room. He sat down besides me. He started groping me. I knew what he was trying to do, but I thought that maybe if I played it off, then he would just go away. His groping became more intense.

He asked everybody to get out of the room as he lay on top of me. I asked them to get him off of me. I tried to get up and follow everyone else into the other room. But my friends got up, turned off the light and closed the door. He snatched the phone from me and hung it up.

He started kissing me while trying to take off my pants at the same time. I called for my sister and my friends, but no one came into the room. I couldn't believe it was happening again. I had lived my entire life trying to avoid this scene again.

They didn't help me. He managed to take my pants off. I closed my legs as tight as I could, but he was much stronger than I was. He placed his feet between my ankles and pushed my legs apart. He raped me.

My cry became a faint whimper. There was no longer a need to scream. No one wanted to hear me cry. My friends helped him rape me. God allowed him to rape me.

When he was done, he got up, pulled up his pants and left. I sat lifeless in the dark.

Hating my life. Hating me.

I didn't have the energy to put my pants back on. I sat in the dark--naked and ashamed. I had been in this place before. Five years had passed since my first violation and here I was again— older, stronger and yet weaker. "How could I have allowed this to happen again?" I thought to myself. Why did people want to hurt me?

What was I supposed to do now? I didn't call the police. They wouldn't have believed me. I was trapped. I was crushed. I was lost. My life song had been wounded- outcast- orphan- rejected- despised and still it sang. Would I ever escape the claws of the enemy? How could I fight something I couldn't see? How could I stand against the unseen forces that were destroying my life?

Crazo won that night. He scored and I paid the price. I resolved that night while I lay on the floor in a darkened, rape-stenched room that I could still be better. I would be better. I would be better than every low-life who sought to torment me. I would be better than every person who spoke or thought less of me. I would be better than a friend who lets a friend get raped.

I resolved that I would fight back. Only thing is—I didn't know how to fight back. I was tired of fighting—throwing punches into thin air. My swings landed nowhere. I could use my education but that hadn't and couldn't stop the attacks. I was still vulnerable. Part of me wanted to give up the idea that there was any good in the world. I stopped wondering what wrong I had done to others.

I wondered what wrong I had done to God. Why did he hate me so much? I couldn't grasp his so-called "love". It seemed to come with hurt, rape, molestation, abuse, and rejection attached. If that were God's idea of love I wondered what hate would look like.

I figured that I would suck it up and roll with the punches. There was nothing I could do to change the events that had taken place, nor could I prevent them.

My tears became fury. I would never drop another tear over anything that ever happened to me. I was tired of crying. In my opinion, crying meant weakness. It meant that I was weak.

No matter how bad things looked or felt, I still hoped that things would one day get better. I guess you could've called me an optimist or you could've called me crazy. Either way, I wanted to believe—I had to believe there was a better life waiting for me somewhere. If I failed to believe it--hope was gone.

One day I'd want to commit suicide and then the next day I'd want to live. I battled with the issue of living every day. The only thing that kept me holding on was not only hope but also the life I wanted to create for my kids. I couldn't kill myself. I wasn't going to leave the world to protect my kids. I was their protector. They were my responsibility and no one was ever going to hurt them the way I had been hurt.

The only choice I had was to keep moving. I had to keep holding on. I had survived so much already. I knew that I could survive anything. Nothing would break me—any more.

So, I put on my fake face and fought my way through. I went to school everyday with my kids in mind. I hoped that one day I would be a good mother and that one day I would be a better me.

In the blink of an eye
The atmosphere changed
Life tragedies disintegrated
Circumstances rearranged...
An appearance into my life
A stranger came to be
Drawing me into a world
Of freedoms and realities...
No longer wishing
Hoping to be heard
Mirrored by her compassion
Sheltered by her words...
Whispering her existence
Into my soul and mind
Praying, believing for me
Experiencing the Ultimate
Encounter of a Lifetime...

~ Chapter 7 ~

Experience of a Lifetime

It's often been said that friends come into your life for a reason, a season or a lifetime. They've said that the season could extend for several days, several months, several years or the rest of one's life.

Only God knows the reasons he brings people into your life. Some have gone as far as believing that many of the friends we encounter aren't friends at all, but are angels sent to earth to teach us. I've had my fair share of angel experiences but I wanted something someone in my life that was tangible and trustworthy. God sent a special person into my life to fulfill the need.

He sent her to guide me in the direction of my destiny. My past left its imprint on my behavior, self-esteem and thoughts. I walked around with immorality, injustice and insecurity in my backpack. Everything that had happened dictated my decisions.

I grew up in a home that emphasized abuse, shame, and the lie that I was worth nothing more than a $1 dollar bill. I believed that I was a mistake either. I believed that no one wanted me. Not my mom, my dad and not even God.

These lies left me searching for the love, acceptance and protection in the wrong places

What was I searching for?

I was searching for love, acceptance and my place in this world. I found myself hurt time and time again. As soon as the pain subsided I'd forget the impact the hurt would bring and I'd repeat the same thing over hoping the second time around would be better. I thought that there was no way out of this cycle of defeat.

I was confused about a lot of things. Nothing made sense to me. If love was good, then why was I being hurt? I was a victim of mixed messages. I confused love with sex—no surprise there. It felt good to be touched in that way.

That love felt better than no love at all. I was being used and there was nothing I could do about it. My self-esteem was non-existent. I saw myself just as everyone else had my entire life. I was ugly, stupid, and worthless. After all that's all I was ever told. I became engulfed in fear, promiscuity and eventually pregnancy.

I was set up to fail—and I did. I was in the ninth grade and pregnant with my second child. I wasn't the only girl pregnant in my school nor was I the only one who had kids, but I was the youngest and I was the most talked about.

Everyone, students and teachers, talked about my messy life. They talked about me like they knew me. They didn't know me but they assumed they did. They accused me of being a slut, whore, and every other word they could think of.

By this time I was use to hearing those words and I was used to being talked about. As much as I tried to not let it affect me—it did. I put on a big smile everyday just to make it through the hurtful comments.

I walked the halls of my high school ashamed. I could've kicked myself for being pregnant again. I just couldn't figure out how I had gotten here again.

I hated my life. All of my life I had believed what others had to say about me. I drank the water that contaminated my soul.

I walked in fear. I feared fear. I feared rejection. I feared acceptance. I feared love and I feared never having love. I feared failure and I feared success.

There was nothing worth living for except my sons—who I figured would hate me if they were old enough to know who I was.

People may have talked about hell, but I was living it on earth. I lived hell every time I walked the halls and heard the whispers of my tormentors.

Their venom sucked what life I had left out of me. Suicide was on my mind more than my next meal. I was too afraid to go with it but I wanted to die. I feared dying because it was unknown. What if it was worse than being alive? I was stuck in two worlds: hell and hell on earth.

Every girl who was pregnant and every boy who had a child was called down to the school library for a meeting. We walked in one by one asking each other why we were being called to this meeting. What was this meeting about anyway? As we entered the room we saw a circle of chairs placed in the center of the room. There was a tall, white lady greeting us all at the door. She gave a warm welcome as we each entered and then commanded that we each take a seat in one of the chairs.

It didn't take long to figure out what was going on. I glanced over the room and saw every girl with a protruding stomach and their boyfriends—only a few had boyfriends—most had walked away when they found out about the pregnancy.

 The room was filled with pregnant teens and I was one of them. I thought to myself—"Oh, great, I'm here to hear a lecture on how to stop having sex and never get pregnant again."

 We each sat in a chair. The white lady closed the door and took a seat in the last empty chair. Her eyes roamed the room—making contact with each of us. Surely, this white lady can't tell us about teenage pregnancy. She didn't know us as teens and she didn't know us minorities. Her world was different, but I thought I'd at least give her a chance to make a fool of herself.

 She opened by stating her name and that she was the teen facilitator for our district. She asked each of us to state our name, our age, our current grade and the number of children that we had. We went around the room hearing everybody's short description of their lives. Everyone smiled at the person speaking as to give him/her an unspoken sign of encouragement. Then it was my turn. I tried to speak as loudly as I could. My name is Latoya Marcus. I'm in the ninth grade and I'm pregnant with my second child. "Daaaaang," they belted simultaneously.

I was crushed by their response. I faked a smile and sucked back the tears. These punks weren't going to make me cry. I had cried enough in my lifetime. But I was ashamed. I was an outcast among outcasts. How was I any different from any of them? We were all in the same predicament.

I didn't get an affirming smile or encouraging nod. I could hear them whisper to each other—some even laughed. One girl shouted, "Dang, when I was your age I was playing with Barbie dolls." I wanted to fight back. I wanted to tell her that she left Barbie alone because she started playing with Ken. But I didn't say anything. I sat in silence.

What gave them the right to criticize me when they had done the same thing? It's human nature, I guess. Kick those who are down. Make sure they stay lower than you.

I could see everyone's mouth gaped open. I saw how many clasped their hands over their mouths to hold back their laughter or their judgment. They were all shocked and now they had their ammunition. They had someone lower than them. They were ridiculed because of their pregnancies and I was rejected because of mine. I wasn't like them after all. I was still different.

The white lady, Kathy Jimerson, didn't say a word. Her eyes were locked on me. She just watched. It took all the strength I could muster to look her dead in her eyes and not cry. It was her fault I was an outsider again. She should've minded her own business. It was too late though. Everyone knew my life.

Kathy chimed in to calm the room. She began her little spiel about the purpose of the meeting. She was starting a teen pregnancy support program in our school. It was going to be a group for teen parents--a group where we could talk about our experiences. I figured after what just happened I wouldn't be sharing mine for a while.

It wasn't long after our first meeting when we started meeting in our TAPS (Teens As Parents and Students) groups. To my amazement everyone was pretty nice. I guess they forgot about our first meeting, which was cool, because I wanted to forget that that day ever happened.

We all had a story to tell and we were thankful that she provided the environment. I learned valuable life lessons in the groups.

Many of the girls were having sex. They just either didn't get pregnant or had abortions, yet they'd come to the meetings and judge others. Many of them had family support. Some had both a mom and dad at home. Some still had their baby daddies around.

No one had lived the life I had lived and was living. They were fortunate to have people in their lives that cared about them.

Sadly, they took things for granted. They thought that the group was a joke. I took it serious. I had nothing to lose and too much to gain.

Kathy and I got to know each other pretty well over the years. But the road was long and hard. I was guarded and closed off to the entire world, including her. I had been so beaten down that I couldn't take another hit. I wasn't going to take another hit. If I did, it would be over my dead body—literally.

I rejected every motion she made to draw near to me. I wanted her to stay away and I wanted her to draw near. I wanted her to see my fury, but I needed her to see my pain. There was a breakthrough storming. It would be more than I could handle at the time, but it was the breaking point for my healing.

I had met with Kathy several times in individual counseling sessions. I thought nothing of it when one of the counselor's aides came into the classroom and told me Kathy wanted to speak with me in the child development classroom. Even though I had met with her before I was nervous for some reason about this session.

I entered the room and found Kathy sitting at one of the tables. She had a polite smile on her face but something was definitely on her mind. I was tempted to turn around. There was tension in the air and I didn't like it. Fear gripped my heart. I just knew she was about to let me down, but what was about to happen in that room would change my life forever.

I sat down in the chair directly across from her--putting as much distance as I could between us. I made sure we didn't make eye contact. I didn't want her to see my shame not to mention my pain. But she did. She had noticed and here we were.

I blocked out much of what she had to say until she struck a nerve. She told me that she had watched an Oprah Winfrey show several days past and it was said that "when something doesn't make sense—question it." So, she took it upon herself to question my life.

She wanted to question why a 14 year-old girl had two children. She knew something was wrong but couldn't pinpoint the problem. She was on the right track more than she knew at the time and more than I could understand.

Finally someone saw me. Someone was finally looking beyond my circumstance and was seeing me--the real me. I didn't want her to though. It was safer inside the closet.

"How old were you when you were molested?" she asked.

The room all of a sudden became deathly still. I could almost hear the world on its tiptoes waiting for me to respond. Would I speak, would I remain quiet or would I lie? My heart hit the floor. I felt like dying—all over again.

I contemplated lying. She had invaded my privacy. She and Oprah Winfrey had no right. They didn't know me. They didn't know my story. Besides, the molestation was my dirty little secret. No one was supposed to know. As hard as I tried to shake it off and pretend the question was never asked, my tears gave me away--I didn't have to answer.

Everything she said before or after that was a blur. The room seemed surreal. My chest muscles tightened around my heart. It seemed like I was going to have a heart attack. I didn't say a word. I kept my head down and tried not to cry. It didn't work. I couldn't control the tears that rolled over my eyes and onto the table.

They slid down my face in streams, hitting the table like little raindrops. Each drop carried the pain I had carried for so long.

The years of locked up pain from my past flowed out that day. I could no longer hide. I had been discovered and I could do nothing about it. I was uncovered. I didn't know what to say or do. Time had frozen. My heart was pounding. I could feel every beat against my chest.

In those days I could fake a smile better than anyone. I'd put on the façade that everything was okay. I pretended to be happy all the time. No one was ever going to see me sweat, cry or break. My smile was my defense mechanism. It protected me from the elements of life. Smiles confuse people. They don't know how to read them so they leave you alone—assuming that all is well. I liked it that way. I liked being left alone. It was easier that way.

Kathy opened the closet door on my secret. With all of my being I wanted to run out of the school. I couldn't fake it anymore. My smile had faded and now I had to tell someone about the shame I had carried for so many years.

I told her about the abuse and I cried. That's all that I remember about that day--I cried. A lot of time crying is good for the soul. It's supposed to bring healing and peace. Not for me. Crying opened up an emotion I longed to forget. My past was now staring me in the face. I realized it was never going to let me go.

Kathy reached across the table and touched my hand. She told me that God loved me and that he had a plan for my life. She told me that God didn't cause the abuse and that he cared about me. Even though I wanted to rebel against her statements, I knew that what she was saying was true. It was the truth that my grandmamma taught me.

For many years I thought God was mad at me for being molested and having sex. I was just as mad at him as he was at me. While Kathy was speaking to me about the love that God had for me I flashed back to the time the angel came to my Grandmamma's house. God sent me an angel. Better late than never.

I don't remember much about the rest of the session. I do remember getting up from the table feeling like my whole world was falling apart—again. I had lost control. I was no longer in control of my life. Something strange had happened.

The walk back to class seemed like an eternity. The hallways seemed to never end. Instead of going back to class I went into one of the bathrooms so I could get myself together—so I could fall apart.

I was lost and confused, as had always been the case. I didn't know if everything that had just happened was good or bad. Was I going to be judged? Was I going to be in trouble? Was she going to spread my business all over the school?

    I walked down the hall in a daze. I was filled with anger. Thoughts were racing through my mind at record speed. Who was this self-righteous white lady telling me about my life? What did she know? Who cared that she heard Oprah talk about sexual abuse? Oprah didn't know me. She didn't know me. What gave her the right to "question" my life?

    I went into the girls' bathroom and I fell apart. The emotions were too strong for me to control. I couldn't hold them in. I went into one of the stall, closed the door and silently cried. I didn't want another student to come in and see me in that condition. I had enough trouble to worry about. I didn't need anybody else in my business.

    I sat down on the toilet seat in silence. That day was bitter sweet. I had wanted to tell someone for years, but I wanted no one to know. I wanted to be protected and yet I wanted to be left alone. I didn't want them to blame me for what had happened. I thought that perhaps it was my fault. Maybe I had turned him on in some sick way.

I wanted to stay locked away in the closet of shame and desperation and I wanted someone to care enough to unlock the door. Kathy did just that. She unlocked the door and there I sat on a toilet seat in the girls' bathroom trying to figure out what it all meant and what I had to do next.

I borrowed my value from my abusive past. I was intoxicated on rejection, abandonment and fear. I drank the words of perverted love. I was empty. I was looking for someone to fill me with something other than dirt.

Since the time I was born I had been searching for just one person to love me. Because of the abuse I had a different view of what that love looked like. I did the best I could. I had pursued my own definition of love and still didn't know what it meant. Lust was poured out onto me and lust is what I pursued. I tried to fill my empty withering soul with sex. The more I drank the thirstier I became.

I found hope during those years though. Kathy came into my life and told me I was valuable. She clung to me like white on rice—no pun intended. Her demonstration of love and compassion motivated me to see life in the future instead of the past replaying over and over again. Kathy was determined to see me make it.

For the first time in my life I had someone who cared—and it was scary. I didn't know what to do with the love she began to show. It felt good to have someone care. At the same time it was a road I long ago resolved to rebuke.

I reminded myself to never put trust in anyone regardless of what they had done. I would care for me. I lied to myself. I did need her, more than I knew at the time.

We never spoke much about the abuse after that day. I knew that she knew and that's all I needed. She knew and she cared. I no longer wanted to be a victim of circumstance, but I didn't know how to get free.

For many years I had placed a shell around my heart, my mind and my spirit. I blocked the world out. I didn't think it had much to offer me anyway. It would take years for the healing to unravel. My goal at this time was to just work on being free.

Kathy created a platform for the group to tell middle school students about our lives. We didn't want them to become "like us." We traveled to schools and spoke about our experiences with teen pregnancy. We gave the gory details of our lives—making sure to leave nothing to the imagination. It was an awesome experience. It was one that would shape me for the rest of my life.

I was always the last to speak. That was Kathy's plan. She often told me I was the most powerful speaker and that I had a message the world needed to hear. That's when my healing began. It began during those speaking engagements. From all I had gone through I had the opportunity to help someone else and that made me feel valuable. I had something to contribute to society.

Borrowed Water

I spoke about the abuse and how it affected my life. I'd glance over the audience and see many girls and boys began to cry. Kathy unlocked my shame and now I was unlocking theirs. There was hope. I could see it and I could taste it.

After each session students would approach me in tears and tell me about the abuse they had suffered or were suffering. I led them to the counselors so they could get the help they needed.

Lives were being changed because I was speaking out about my abuse just like mine had been changed because Oprah spoke about hers.

I couldn't believe I was making a difference. Me, the bald-headed, molested, raped, black girl who had two kids.

Through the fire
Neglected by rain
Succumbed to dehydration
Embraced by shame...

Enduring abuse
Shame and lies
Hiding from the death
I feel inside...

Hope is on the horizon
Change slowly comes
Relief from the torture
Of fire, coals and stones...

Sheltered, protected
Strengthened my soul
Brought through the fire
Perhaps one day made whole...

~ Chapter 8 ~

Through The Fire

Some time later, my family moved to California. I stayed behind because I wanted to finish high school. I had just completed my junior year and was getting ready for graduation. My two sons and I moved in with the father of my second child and his family in the summer of 1993.

We lived in a two-bedroom. There were twelve of us crammed into an apartment. Richard and I slept on the floor in the living room and my kids slept on the couch.

It wasn't a move I wanted to make but had no choice. I had nowhere else to go. Living with him was hell. He took abuse to another level. I didn't know I could be beat so low. I had lived in a rough world and I had survived. I was a strong, determined young woman, but I was no match for what he was about to bring.

He was very abusive. I endured emotional, verbal, and physical abuse, from him calling me bitches, hoes to slapping and choking me and tossing me over trashcans. I was forced to endure the abuse because I had no place else to go.

I knew for years that he had an abusive personality. I had seen him with other girls. I had heard about him beating up his girlfriends, but until this time he had never done anything to me. I thought I was safe. Based on my past experience I should've known I wouldn't be.

The first few weeks were okay. Things were pretty calm. The only problem we had between us was his unemployment. He had just been released from jail after serving an eight-month sentence for aggravated robbery and selling crack.

He had been a drug dealer since the day we met. That was his occupation. I didn't like the lifestyle that drugs brought and I was scared of jail.

When he got out he was placed on probation and was forced to get a job. He eventually got a job at Captain D's, but quit after working only two weeks. Back to drugs he went.

He never got another job. He had a lot of time on his hands to do nothing. I saw that he didn't want much out of life and I did, so I went and got a job to take care of my kids. I started working for Grandys', a southern style restaurant. Grandys' was a one-mile walk from where we lived. I walked every step of that mile by myself. I'd walk to work in the blazing sun and I'd walk home in the midnight hour.

Richard stayed home and watched the kids while I went to work. He didn't care if I made it to work safely. I was on my own. He and his friends sat around all day and smoked weed when they could get some.

One day as I was coming home from work, one of my neighbors stopped me. She had news to tell me. She told me that Richard had been cheating on me with several girls in the apartment complex.

I didn't care about his behavior at the time because I was on a mission--a mission to graduate from high school and a mission to provide stability for my kids. I couldn't get caught up in his life.

I didn't need him or his lifestyle getting in my way, but I didn't want to look stupid in front of everybody either, so I confronted him with the information and all hell broke loose. It was just a matter of time before everything he had been doing would be revealed.

I later found out that he had been sleeping with my neighbor. She brought him dinner at night. We had a lot of fights over his escapades but nothing ever changed. As a matter of fact they got worse.

One day I was cooking dinner. We were all sitting around a beautiful Saturday afternoon relaxing. Richard's mom and uncles were playing cards at the table when the front door opened when in walked Richard and his female friend.

Everyone's mouths hit the floor. He had the audacity to bring another woman into the house. His family became indignant and started yelling at him. He sat down on the couch and smirked. It was my turn to say something.

All eyes were on me. What was I going to say? Was I going to put up with this? The answer to that question was "no". I started walking towards him. He jumped up and hurriedly took his female friend outside. At this point I was fed up. I walked outside to go the phone booth to find somewhere else to live and I saw him kissing his female friend. I hated him for treating me that way but I couldn't get out and he knew it. Things still got worse.

One day a few friends and I were outside talking and hanging out. He pulled up in the car with his sister's boyfriend. He got out of the car walked up to me and slapped me. For no reason at all he just slapped me. He slapped me so hard that his fingernail got caught in my skin. He left a three-inch slash across my face. Then he grabbed me by the throat and started choking me. I tried to hit him several times but that didn't work. He had a grip on my neck and was not about to let go.

His sister's boyfriend was finally able to get him off of me. He walked away laughing. I stood in the parking lot shocked ad embarrassed. My friends didn't say a word. They left and I went inside the house to clean up the blood dripping from my face.

I still had nowhere to go so I stayed. When I wasn't at work, I was at home cooking, cleaning or reading. Falling into a good book was my way of escaping the present. One afternoon after I fed the kids and cleaned the house, I lay down on the couch to read. I was the only in the house at time. It was peaceful for a change and I welcomed the silence.

A few minutes after I sat down Richard walked in with a friend. He approached me lying on the couch and slapped me again. He spouted off something about me cheating on him. I immediately jumped up and ran outside toward the telephone booth. I was trying to call someone to come get me. I had had it and it didn't matter where I lived at that point. Of all the things I thought I was, a punching bag was not going to be one of them.

He caught up with me at the phone. He picked me up and tossed me over the trashcan. He told me "if I ever catch you cheating I'll kill you bitch" I lay on the ground crying--that familiar place on the ground. My life had always seemed to make sure I ended up in the same position—on my back.

Relief came shortly thereafter. He was arrested for selling dope again. His time in jail brought some well-needed relief. I continued to work and by September I was in school. I had made it to my senior year. I was making progress—slowly but surely.

We all eventually moved into a four-bedroom house in the black neighborhood. I finally had my own room. I was going to school. I was working. I was raising my kids. I was happy. Things were looking up. That was until Richard was released from jail. I did forgive him for all he had done and was happy to see him. The smile on my face wouldn't last long.

He seemed to have changed. And he had for the most part. He didn't hit me anymore. He stopped calling me names. Things were better, but he still didn't get a job. He was living off my wages.

Even though he still had no vision for his life I had vision for mine. I was on my way out and I wasn't going to let anybody stop me.

Pregnant Again!

Dang, what was I thinking? For the past four years I had Kathy and other teachers tell me that sex outside of wedlock was wrong. I never knew what wedlock or sin meant but they had something to do with each other. I had attended child development classes for years. I spent countless hours in support groups. I had even told middle school students that sex was not fun.

Yet, here I was pregnant again—for the third time. I didn't care what anyone else thought about me. I did, however, care what Kathy would think. I had made a mess of my life without even trying. I wanted so much from my life and now I had a third baby to care for.

I was disappointed in myself. Surely I should've known that sex would cause me to get pregnant. I just couldn't tell Richard no. I was living with his family and felt obligated to be with him. I felt that since we already had one child together that it was best for me to try to make it work. I made it with two kids and I could make it with three. I was still determined to make something of myself in spite of the circumstances that were occurring.

I continued to work at Grandys'. My walk was now about a mile and a half. I'd go to school, -- catching the bus at 6 a.m.--come home from school at 4, change my clothes and walk to work by 5. I worked until about 11 or 12 at night and walked home. The walk home was pretty scary. I lived in the "hood" so everything located between the job and the walk home was prostitutes, pimps, drug dealers and dope fiends. I wasn't afraid of them. I was used to seeing them. I was afraid of the countless white men who would follow me home in their cars.

All I could do was sing Sunday school songs to keep my mind off the perverts. I prayed and asked God to keep me safe. These men would follow me all the way until I reached my front door. God must've heard my prayers because I always made it home safely.

Richard never made sure that I made it to and from work safely. He had his mind on other things than my safety. He had his mind on women and drugs that he was no longer selling but using.

A few months after getting out of jail, Richard had made his mark in my life in many ways. The abuse that he dished out before he went to jail was nothing compared to what he did when he was released.

I was seven months pregnant when I found out that Richard got one of our neighbors pregnant. She was six months pregnant at the time. I was devastated. Even though he had a history of cheating—it still hurt. I had convinced myself that he was redeemable and that I was the one who would bring him to "the light."

Regardless of the abuse, I continued to believe in the best. I allowed myself to be abused over and over again because I didn't have the power to say "no more". I was used to being used and mistreated.

Each time he lied, cheated, hit me, or cursed me out I forgave him. I believed that one day my "kind heart" would help him see that there was a better way. He never did.

Everyone in the house and in the neighborhood knew he had been cheating--everybody but me. If nothing else in my life could break me--that did it. I was at my breaking point. I couldn't take anymore. If life wanted me to be defeated then I was ready to give in.

Change came a lot sooner that I imagined. Richard was arrested for robbing a convenience store. He was given 30 years in the state penitentiary. He was going to be gone for a long time. In spite of all he had done, I still felt sorry for him. I wished things could've turned out differently for him. I believed he was a good person deep, deep, deep down inside. I thought I could bring the best out in him and I was going to do just that—somehow.

    Several months after Richard was locked up, I met my dad. Richard's mom worked at a catfish shack. I went to the shack to visit her one-day. When I opened the door a lady was coming out.

    "Hey baby, what's your mamma's name"

    I reluctantly whispered, "Gloria."

    "You're supposed to be my brother's daughter, I'm your aunt Jackie,"

    I smiled and said "okay". She hugged me and then she left.

    A few days later, Richard's mom called me at home and told me to come to the restaurant—there was someone who wanted to meet me. I had no idea who she was talking about. Who wanted to meet me? When I got to the restaurant there was an elderly lady sitting in the corner booth. Richard's mom told me that the lady in the corner was my grandmother. It turned out that the lady who hugged me a few days prior was my aunt. After she saw me, she went home and told her mother that she had seen me. My grandmother wanted to see me for herself. I spent several hours with her that day.

A few days after my meeting with her, my dad showed up at my front door. To say I was surprised would be an understatement. I had been waiting for this moment my entire life. I often dreamt about the day I would see him face-to-face. I had even role-played the way that I would ask him all the questions I ever had.

My dreams were finally answered. He was now standing right before my eyes and I didn't have a word to say. I was excited he had found me, but I was afraid that he would do what he did 17 years ago and leave. I was upset it took him 17 years to find me but relieved that the man I had fantasized about for 17 years was now a reality.

I invited him into the house and he took a seat. We didn't have much to say to each other. I didn't probe him with a thousand questions. At that point the reason that he left didn't matter anymore. My need for a daddy was long gone but I was still curious about this man named Charlie.

We chatted about everything but the main thing. I guess neither one of us wanted to break the ice on that subject. I told him that I was in my senior year, I was pregnant, I was about to graduate and I had two kids. I was waiting for him to say something negative so I could give him a piece of my mind. But he didn't say anything negative. He only asked me if I needed anything. I lied and told him no.

He stayed for a short while. He got up to leave after about thirty minutes. When he got to the door he reached his hand towards me. I looked down and noticed that he had money in his hand. I immediately flashed back to the one-dollar I was given to keep my mouth shut about the molestation.

In my eyes, my dad was doing the same thing my mom's boyfriend had done. He tried to appease me by giving me money. I guess he hoped the money would correct his wrong and help me forget that he abandoned me. I looked at the money for a second time, declined his offer and shut the door.

I didn't know what the future held for me. I knew that things were changing but didn't know the affects that the changes would have on me. All the hopes and dreams I had for my father were crumbled as I faced reality. He didn't want me and he was no better than any other man who had ever been in my life.

I had hit a major wall. I couldn't take another hit. I had to face reality, I was finally defeated. There were too many things happening at the same time. It was more than my heart and mind could take. I was truly broken.

My heart burned within my chest. I wanted to kill myself. I even thought about killing my kids and then killing myself. I didn't want them to live life without me. I didn't want them to endure a childhood like men. If change didn't come I wasn't going to make it.

Thoughts of my life played in my mind over and over again--thoughts of the sexual abuse--the rape--the rejection-- the fears-- the physical and emotional abuse-- the cheating. I was being tormented every night. I was going crazy. When all these thoughts bombarded my mind I would hear my Grandmamma's stories.

I could hear her tell me how good God was. I would hear Kathy tell me that God loved me and wanted a better life for me. I would hear the Sunday school songs we sang at Mr. Dominic's church. I would remember the voice of God I used to hear as a little girl when I would find quiet places to talk to Him.

I needed a change and I needed it fast. I was so desperate for someone to love me once and for all. I lost all hope. All the fight I possessed was gone. Life was too strong for me. It was too much for me to handle. I could no longer see past the pain. Enough was enough.

One Sunday morning I got up and walked four blocks to one of the many churches in my neighborhood. I went in and sat down. I didn't want to sing. I didn't want to hear any preaching. All I needed was the God of my Grandmamma. If he didn't intervene then I wouldn't make it. I was at the end of my ropes—the same ropes that I would hang from if God didn't help me.

    At the end of service I found myself at the altar with my arms raised in the air. Like a broken water line the tears uncontrollably ran down my face. I cried out for God to help me. I didn't know about all that religious stuff. I just needed a miracle or I was going to die. I needed the pain to go away. I needed God to help me. I had two kids to raise and a third one on the way.

    Whatever happened at that altar changed my life. As I walked the four blocks back home that day, I cried as I'd never cried before. This time these were tears of joy. It felt like I was walking on clouds. Every burden seemed to have been lifted. My spirit, my mind and my body were different. I was clean. I was new. I had my fight back.

I graduated a month later from high school. I was a high school graduate. I beat the odds. They said I couldn't do it and I did. They said that I wouldn't do it and I did. They were wrong about me. They pegged me as nothing.

I was somebody and they were just getting a taste of what a "somebody" I would be one day.

Out of everything that happened to me during this time could've destroyed my life. I wanted to quit. I almost did. Hope must've been lingering somewhere in the midst of the chaos. It wouldn't let me go and I was thankful for that. I wasn't strong enough to stop the abuse or the pain that came my way—at least not on my own.

I had been through the fire and now I was going to be walking in the rain. The water of God's presence snuffed out the fires that were burning me alive. Now, I had God to help me. I was on my way to being the "me" I was created to be. I would be stronger and more hopeful than ever. I was on my way to a new life.

Change is brewing
Scent lingers in the air
The smell of victory
Flowing through the cares...

Purging the fear
Eliminating the shame
Changing perspectives
Redeeming the pain...

Change is welcome
Faith is seeded
Change is coming
Faith is needed

~ Chapter 9 ~

Change Is Coming

After my third son came I moved into my own apartment. My mom's boyfriend died, so she moved back to Texas. It felt good to be around my own family for a change. They were a breath of fresh air compared to the life I had lived with Richard. God was slowly restoring my relationships.

My mom was now different than she was in the past. I had compassion for her. I knew what it felt like to almost find love and then have it snatched away.

I had nothing when I moved into my apartment. All I had was my children, my God, a twin sized mattress and a radio. I was more than happy in my apartment. I didn't care what I didn't have. I was thankful for the things that I did have.

    I kept in contact with Kathy after my graduation. She knew that I had moved into my own place. I thought she would've never wanted to see me again after the embarrassment I caused by getting pregnant again. But Kathy did more than just forgive me—she loved me even harder. She had been a teen parent—we later found out—and she knew what I was going through to some extent.

    Kathy didn't give up on me. Her belief in me was critical. I thought that she would give up on me after she found out that I was pregnant. I thought she was going to kick me out of the group. After all, she had gone to bat for me in so many ways and I disappointed her. I was sorry for that but there was nothing that I could do to change what had happened. So, I waited for her rejection. I believed that surely it would come. Surely she would do what everyone else had done in my life—leave.

Change is Coming

I was sure she'd kick me out of the group and focus on helping the kids that didn't do what I did. But she didn't. If she had, then she would've fallen into the category of everybody else in my life—liars. I expected rejection but I got forgiveness and love instead.

Kathy came to my apartment one day so we could catch up with each other. We sat on my living room floor and talked about the changes occurring in my life. I told her about my experience at the church that day. I told her how I gave my life to Jesus Christ and how things were changing for me. Things weren't perfect but they were better. She agreed.

A few weeks later there was a knock on my door. I was washing dishes. I dried off my hands and answered the door. It was Kathy and her husband. She asked if she could come in. She and her husband stepped into the apartment. She told me she had told her church about me and that they had all come to bring me furniture.

I couldn't understand what she meant by "all" because she and her husband Phil were the only two people in my apartment. She asked me to follow her outside. I couldn't believe my eyes. There were about twenty people outside with cars and trucks loaded with furniture. I had never felt so much love before. I cry every time I recount this story.

There were bunk beds for the boys, a crib for my baby and a bed for me. There were couches, sheets, toiletries, dishes, and tables. One day I had nothing and the next day I had an apartment filled with furniture. I couldn't believe what was happening. I was overwhelmed. These people didn't even know me and yet they loved me like no one ever had.

They did more than just bring me furniture. They set everything up. The men put together the bunk bed and set up my kitchen table. The women put sheets on the beds and put all the dishes in the cabinets. After everything was set up they brought boys and me into the living room. These white men took my black children in their arms and prayed over them.

I finally understood what love meant and how it looked.
Only heaven will be able to tell of the love that was shown that day. When everyone left I fed my boys and put them to bed. After they were asleep I ran up and down my hallway thanking God. I felt like He had taken my face in His hands and kissed me with a thousand kisses. I fell to my knees crying. I couldn't believe it. God loved me and he loved on me. God did send angels after all.

This was just the beginning of my new life. I had a lot to learn and a lot to unlearn. I spent the next several years taking care of my kids and attending church. I spent countless hours reading my Bible and praying. I wanted to know God to the fullest extent possible. My dad was in my life but he was still distant. That was okay because at least I knew him now. At least my void had been filled.

Even though things were changing I still had issues. Victory hadn't come yet. I had learned abuse and rejection my entire life and it would take more than a church service to change that. I would eventually pass down the abuse I suffered as a child.

I hate to admit that I was an abusive mother. I spanked my kids every day. I didn't beat them, but a day didn't go by that they didn't get a spanking for something. I often got in their faced and yelled at them. I intimidated them with my size and voice. I threw things around to scare them.

As much as I regret what I did it was all I knew. I didn't know how to be a good mother. I cared and loved my kids very much, but I needed to learn to love me so I could give them the best of me. They deserved a healthy mom.

I found myself screaming at them everyday. I was an eighteen year-old mother of three children. I was overwhelmed and ignorant of how to love. I was willing to learn. I wanted to be better at living than I had been in the past.

I went to God for help. I asked Him to show me how to love the little lives He blessed me with. I prayed that He would help me see them the way He saw them. Change didn't happen overnight, it would take time. God had his work cut out for him. I was a mess—a hot mess.

It had always been my dream to attend college, but I didn't have a car nor did I have the means to buy one. I started saving my $226 monthly welfare check to buy a car. My rent was $13 dollars a month. I was receiving food stamps so I didn't have to worry about food. I mentioned to Kathy my plans to Kathy. I wanted her to see that I was making progress and that I was determined to make something out of my life.

Needless to say Kathy saved the day once again. She and Phil bought me a car. It was a red 1987 Chevrolet Cavalier. It was in mint condition. God provided a way out of no way. I was on my way to college. I enrolled at a community college and started taking classes toward my Associates degree in Liberal Arts. I didn't know what that meant but it sounded good and I wanted to sound good for once in my life. Change was occurring but it wouldn't manifest for many years.

Even though Richard had put me through so much I still loved him. I remained with him while he was in prison. I thought he was the best I could get. My self-esteem was more than low—it was not existent. I believed that no one would want me. I was used up and I had three kids. No wise man would want to be with a ready-made family.

I spent twelve years of my life locked up with him. I was locked up in my mind. I married him while he was in prison—divorced him several years later—and then married him again. I was trying to be to him what God had been to me—a savior. He didn't change. He was still the same Richard I had always known, but I believed I could bring out the best in him.

Why I married him after all he had done? I wouldn't know that answer for many years. I devoted my entire life to him. I'd travel for hours to visit him all over the state of Texas. One prison was about a seven-hour trip. I made that trip once a month while living on a $226 welfare check.

Change is Coming

    I thought I was obligated to be there for him. I felt sorry for him. He didn't have anybody. I didn't want him to be alone in that place. After all, I told myself time and time again that he could change. I tricked myself into believing that not only did he have the potential to be a better person but also that he just needed my love and attention to make these changes. He'd curse me out in his letters. He'd accuse me of cheating. I allowed him to take me through hell---literary hell. He affected my life more in prison than he did when he was out. I was depressed and gained over 100 pounds. I was thirsty for the genuine love that exists between a man and a woman.

    I'd take long road trips to visit him at the prison. Depending on which unit he was in, I'd travel anywhere from 2 to 7 hours. I was a regular at the prison. He needed my support and that's how a woman supports her man. I was a ride or die chick. I was down with my man. I liked being in the long distance relationship because I had control. I controlled if or when he would see me. I controlled the visitations. Surely, he couldn't hurt me now.

What I was doing was fooling myself. I couldn't change him because I couldn't change me. I wasn't healthy enough to love anyone. I tried and I tried hard, only to fail time and time again. I couldn't imagine that he could do real harm to me. He was locked up and he was limited. I was wrong. The damage he caused while in prison was almost worse than the damage that he caused when he was free.

Waiting twelve years for him was an accomplishment for me. I thought waiting for "nothing" made me a real woman. I was committed and loyal, but I was committed and loyal to the wrong person.

Things would get worse at the same time they were getting better. I was becoming a better person. I was attending church, reading books on how to be a better parent, and helping the people in my neighborhood. How could things go wrong at the same time? The devil didn't want to let go of the grip he had always had on me.

When I say that things went wrong, I don't mean that I suffered another tragedy. My personal life of trying to love a man who was incapable of loving me was tearing me up on the inside.

I stayed with Richard because being with him, even though he was locked up, was better than facing the reality that no one would ever love me. I didn't know what love was or what it felt like.

I equated love with being hurt and suffering. My relationship sang that song. I was hurt and I was suffering and I thought it was love. I could love him without being hurt physically, but I forgot that my emotional and mental states were vulnerable.

During the twelve-year wait, I became extremely depressed. I refused to let anyone know I was depressed because I felt like they didn't care anyway, and I wasn't going to give anyone the opportunity to beat me down more than I had already been. I stuffed my pain and depression on the inside. I suffered in silence. I'd look in the mirror everyday and tell myself "I would not be beaten—I would win".

After looking at myself everyday I failed to take notice of the obvious. Although, I hid my pain from the world, I couldn't hide the effects. I couldn't see the 100 pounds I gained. My pain was manifesting itself in my weight. Not only did I not notice--those around me didn't notice either. If they did they never said anything. I was killing myself with food. It was more than comfort to me. It was my friend.

I had just added another issue to be dealt with on top of everything else on my plate--no pun intended. I lost my identity by taking care of everyone else: my children, my man, my family, my so-called friends and my God. I failed to take care of the most important person in my life—me. I wasn't just a single parent of three children who lived on welfare, but now I was fat. I was sure I could never be loved now. Might as well keep what I had.

Richard was going to spend the next 15 years or so in prison and so would I. I would be locked up in a world where no one could visit--a world of despair, loneliness and self-hatred. I was locked up in my own thoughts of "less than" and I was an inmate of my own soul. I didn't know how I would break free, but I knew that I could and I would.

I was going to be a prisoner to no one—not even myself. I wasn't sure how to get out of the rut, but I knew I'd take one day at a time and give myself a chance to be a better me. Being with Richard was like being locked up in that closet all over again. There wasn't any life in the closet, but I lingered there in hopes of finding something to nourish my deprived soul. I was hungry and thirsty. Even the bitter tasted sweet.

There would be times when I would make the long trip to the prison only to be turned around because he had been in a fight the day before or he had mouthed off to one of the guards or he got caught stealing something. It was always something. So, with my kids in tow, we'd make the long trip back home discouraged. Richard knew we were coming, yet he was not concerned about the effects his behavior had on visitation with his kids. It should've been obvious that he didn't care, but I was blinded by my love for him and my drive to ensure the kids knew him.

I wanted my kids to have a relationship with their dad no matter what. I knew what it felt like to not have my dad around and I didn't want that to happen to them. My oldest son's dad was not involved so having Richard in his life was crucial— I thought. I would suffer whatever I had to suffer to not deprive them of their father.

That was one pain that they would never endure and I was going to make sure of that. Every time I went to the prison they went with me. I'd spend money I didn't have to buy a new outfit for the weekend occasion of sitting on a hot bench at the prison—having each movement watched for two hours. I'd pile on make-up and perfume just so he'd say I was pretty. By the end of the visit most of my make-up would end up on my clothes because of the heat.

    The majority of our weekends were spent in the prison visiting rooms. At times I'd wonder why I was there. I didn't fit in. During the visits I'd glance over the room to see an array of people who all shared a common bond—we were all prison families--victims of society, and most often than not, victims of the ones we were there to see. I'd see a woman, who was probably just like me, trying to hush her crying baby so as not to frustrate the guards or her boyfriend or husband.

    I'd see agitated mothers want to pop their little ones for crying but knowing that discipline in this place was out of the question. I couldn't blame the kids though. It was hard sitting in the same spot for several hours, many times in the hot sun. I wondered if these same kids would return to the prison one day as an inmate instead of a visitor. I thought about this for my own children. How could the cycle be broken?

I would see a young man with tattoos from head to toe crying to his mom about his life there—trying hard to not let anyone see his weaknesses.

Then there were mothers and fathers who made that trip decades to visit their son. I'd watch these men manipulate and con their own parents—having them smuggle cigarettes or drugs past the guards—only to be caught time and time again.

I learned a lot from watching these families. I learned that we were all there desperately hoping and wishing for change. We'd believe the impossible and overlook the obvious--we were hurting and we didn't even know how desperately we hurt.

We couldn't see ourselves past the pain in our own lives. The greatest injustice was not the failed court system or the many men behind bars. The greatest injustice was the lack of love in our lives. I believed this life was the best that I could get. There was an ache in my heart that wouldn't go away. I ached for someone to love me. I ached for me to love me.

Borrowed Water

After many years of crying tears and shedding fears, I realized that I could be more than my own perception. He was with me because I was convenient. I was with him because I was afraid. I knew he was incapable of loving anybody, but being with him was easier than being alone. I could have someone to call my "man" and not have to deal with the realities of not being loved or of being hurt again. I reasoned in my mind that this way was best.

For the time being I was only going to work on one thing at a time. I was going to work on earning my degrees, raising my children to be great men, and learning all I could about God. I was going to take life as it came one day at a time. That's all the energy that I had anyway.

Despair—hopelessness for
A 60 second minute...
I sense hope
But time changes
A bill comes
A bill collector calls
Something breaks
I hate this place

I can't change me

My decisions bind me
I know with my head
I long with my heart
To move to a different place
I feel stuck
I want to cling
I want to push away
I dream to escape the realities of this world

If I could Love me
Where would I be?

~ Chapter 10 ~

If I Could Love Me

The time I spent waiting for Richard had its benefits. It did allow me to focus on more important things without the distractions of a man around. I was able to focus on college, slowly learning to love myself, and raising my kids in a safe home.

I refused to bring any man into the home that would possibly abuse my kids. I didn't want to have sex outside of marriage and end up pregnant like I had done so many times before.

I was tired of things ending up the same way.

I was tired of my messy life.

I lied to myself. I wanted more from a relationship. I wanted to be loved, appreciated, honored and pursued. I wanted to feel like a queen. I wanted to valued and accepted with all my flaws and wounds.

What I wanted, Richard was not able to give. I just couldn't let go though. My insecurities got the best of me. I defended myself against failure by delving myself into school. I loved school but I had secretly made it a way to get acceptance.

The more I achievement meant more acceptance. I worked hard, made good grades and made sure everyone like me. I guess you could've called me a secret people-pleaser. I'd fight against the pressures of life with knowledge. I was proud of how far I had come, but I was still that insecure little girl who was locked up in Grandmamma's closet.

I was strong on the outside and weak on the inside. My identity was locked up in my degrees. When I'd feel inadequate I'd retreat into the education closet. I'd take another class or go to school and sit in the library to escape the pain. School was a way out but now it was my shelter from the fear of failure. I still hadn't learned the art of self-love.

Within two years of attending community college I earned an Associates Degree. I was making strides. Getting this degree increased my desire for knowledge, for education and for life. I enrolled in the University of Texas at Arlington to work on my bachelor's degree in social work. Two years later I walked across the stage.

I did it.

I worked hard and there I was-- a real college graduate.

I accomplished so much and hurt just the same. When I got home the day of my graduation I sat down on the couch and cried. Why cry when I had just graduated from college? I cried because I title to hang on my wall right beside the others--failure, rejection, and nothingness.

I earned a degree but still hadn't found out who I was or what my purpose was. I worked hard just to end up in the same spot—alone. So, to end my identity crisis I enrolled into the Master's program. It was going to take another year to complete and another year to figure out how to love me.

I went from one defense mechanism to another. After I got my degree I struggled even more with my purpose. Time in school was spent lying to myself. I told myself that if I earned one more degree, someone would finally notice me.

I wanted someone to notice what I had to offer the world. I longed to be noticed and accepted for being whom God created. I worked hard to make life pretty on the outside. Only then would no one know the real failure on the inside.

Although a lot of healing had taken place up until this point, the residue from the water poured into my life hadn't been purged. I'd look in the mirror everyday and never liked what I saw. So, I eventually stopped looking in mirrors.

Education was a tool to hide the pain. Despite great strides, I would be of no help to anyone if I didn't learn to help myself on the inside. While education was a great motivator, it didn't fulfill the longing I had for acceptance. It didn't quench my thirst. I found myself thirstier than ever.

My new closet was the four edges of a college degree. It was my salvation and shield from the storms of reality. My smile, my charisma, my intelligence was no match for what I felt on the inside. I felt unworthy of love. I loathed my existence.

It didn't matter how much success I experienced or how many degrees I earned, I still couldn't see past the timid, black girl I saw in the mirror every day.

But along with everything else I had endured and overcome I believed that this too would pass. And it did.

God couldn't heal the pain of my past over night. It would take years of Him cleansing out the grime from the past. I wasn't where I wanted to be but was thankful not to be where I used to be.

I had overcome great obstacles and for that I should've been proud. So much of my life felt empty and so much of my life felt fulfilled.

Though the lives from which I borrowed my destiny left me dry and parched in a deserted land, the smell of rain was in the air. Victory was on its way. Change was brewing. The time for my voice to be heard was echoing among the rain clouds, coming to wash away the destructive thoughts and beliefs I had about myself.

My heart and soul yearned for something more. I longed to know how to move me from victim to victory. God knew the longing that I had. He also knew my every hidden desire, fear, insecurity, regret, rejection and disappointment and he cared about them. He cared about me.

Breakthrough had been occurring in my life. I just couldn't see it because I was so blinded by my past. God was beginning to break every yoke that kept me bound and he began to lift the burdens that life had place upon my shoulders.

I would take care of everyone else yet I neglected me. I would wonder how I was going to make it another day. I'd feel so alone. I'd paint a smile on my face during the day and I'd cry myself to sleep at night.

The burden to live was so strong. I always felt inadequate. It was hard for me to see me. When I looked in the mirror I didn't see beauty—I saw anger, ugliness. I saw a woman who was so powerful and so weak. I locked myself up in the careers, behaviors and slumps that all together never bring fulfillment. We pretend that all is well.

If I could learn to love LaToya, then I could see me the way that God saw me. If I could love me I would see that I was more than a mother, friend, student—I was more than intelligent, nice, motivated and driven.

If I could love me I could realize that I was valuable. I was valuable enough to never have to perform for the audiences in my life again; valuable enough to never drink water from the wells of others and valuable enough to love me beyond old experience, my intellect and all of my rationalizations.

If only I could love me—I would create my own water. I would drink from God's source and not the source from of the people who borrowed their water as well. I wouldn't have to drink my destiny from polluted water sources.
If I could love me there would be no limit to the lives that I could touch—even in my own home.

Learning to love me would be a journey that I was ill prepared to take. Learning to look into the mirror of my life and accept the person that I saw was very hard to do. I had to change my vision.

I had to flush out the words that blurred my vision. I had to reject their lies that I had accepted as truth.

It was time for real change to occur in my life.

Victory came in streams...shinning, flowing~

settling over this charcoaled –skinned

African dream....

    LaToya N. Brown

~ Chapter 11 ~

Look At Me Now

In 2004 rumors were spreading about Richard's sexual behaviors in prison. He was supposedly cheating with the female guards at several of the units. He was deceptive, abusive and stronger and finally believed I deserved better.

I summed everything up with the fact that he was who he had always been. I was the only one to blame for waiting so long.

My insecurities had me in bondage to a man that was searching for his own way to love and acceptance. I now had some major decisions to make. Either I was going to keep putting my life on hold, or I was going to embrace the life I had worked so hard to have.

It was time for me to move on. So, in 2004 I divorced him and began my new life. My life consisted of getting real and getting whole. It was time to love me past my own failures and shortcomings. It was time for me to accept my smile, accept my journey and accept the life I was yet to live.

I graduated from UT Arlington in August 2004. I graduated with my Master's. My hard work finally paid off. My view of education was worth the fight. Instead of being counted most likely to fail—I could now be counted among the few and determined.

Before graduation I had a few more hurdles to jump. My car broke down in the final semester. I was working an internship at a local hospital. After all I had been through; I was not going to let this trial stop me from achieving my goal, so I borrowed a car from a friend. Thank God for her. When I couldn't use her car, I paid others to take me to and from school.

At this point I was still living on welfare. I was still receiving food stamps, Medicaid and TANF. I was also receiving rental assistance from the city. From the outside it looked like things hadn't changed, but never judge a book by the cover. Change takes time. Besides, I had all the patience in the world. I could taste my success.

One month prior to graduation I applied for a job in my hometown school district. I borrowed my friend's van to go to the interview. I teased my friend about her van because it was not only old, but I had to climb in on the passenger's side. If that wasn't enough I had to be careful while driving because the driver's door had been known to fly open while in motion.

I got the job!

God had ordered each step of the way. During this time I also visited car lots. I needed a car and believed I deserved a new one. Time drew near for me to start my new job and I still didn't have a car. I sat down on my couch and had a talk with God. I told God, "I'm sure you didn't give me a job I couldn't get to." Before the words were finish coming from my mouth the phone rang. The Dodge dealership was on the other line.

The salesman told me they were wondering if I was going to come and pick up my car. I had filled out an application but they never indicated whether or not I was approved. Life couldn't have been sweeter. I immediately called up a ride and made my way to get this blessing.

I drove off the lot that day in a 2004 Dodge Stratus. It was mine.

God worked everything out.

Once I reported my employment to the housing authority I was informed that I no longer qualified for rental assistance and I'd have to start paying about $1100 a month in rent. I took that as my cue to look for a house to buy.

I had promised myself that I would be a homeowner by the time I was 30. I told friends about my dream home. I wanted marble and ceramic floors. I wanted a red bedroom with Mahogany wood floors. I wanted wood floors in the boy's bedrooms as well. I mentioned that I wanted marble countertops in the kitchen with thick Venetian blinds. I was just dreaming. I believed that someday I would have all that I ever dreamed about.

Well, I was only 28, but six months after starting my new job I purchased my first home. When I first saw the house before purchasing it my mouth hit the floor. It was everything that I had been talking about—everything.

It had a red bedroom with Mahogany wood floors. This was my home. God heard every word that came from my mouth. He was preparing a place for me.

He has placed me in spacious places. He has opened the door for me to be what he's called me to be—a speaker. Not just because I have a big mouth but I have a story. I have a story I'm not afraid to tell. I'm no longer ashamed or rejected.

I would never lie to you and tell you that life has been a cakewalk from this point. I still have struggles but now I know how to fight right. I have a black belt in overcoming.

I was a young, black girl whose crushed spirit and blurred dreams rose from the ashes and overcame the fires that sought to devour me. I could be more and was determined to have the last say. The world was going to hear my voice.
Hell hath no fury like a little black girl born.

People often ask why I define myself by race.

"Why don't you recognize that you are a woman first?"

I know I'm a woman, but in my eyes I'm a black woman first. For many years I was judged because of my skin. I was made to feel ashamed of my color. I didn't have the opportunity to be proud. I'm glad that through all the trials and hardships I've endured, I have learned to celebrate who I am and to accept who I am.

You've read my story. You've seen how I've overcome every obstacle. "Borrowed Water" has been about showing you that although everyone is not born with a silver spoon in their mouths or Nike tennis shoes on their feet, they can still have the best in life.

The definition of "best" is up to you. This book was written to give you hope. I was inspired to help you move beyond the pain of the past and grasp the future you've longed for – encouraging you to live.

God says He knows what plans He has for us (Ezekiel 29:11). He knows the plans to give us good and not evil, plans to give us a future and a hope. Where was God when my hope for the day was to have food to eat? Where was God when my future was molested and my dreams violated? Where was He—my protector, savior--healer?

Let me tell you where he was. He was on the throne. He was working in my life the entire time. He placed people in my life that fought against the storm. They encouraged me, prayed for me, believed in me and gave me money when I needed it…I wouldn't be where I am today without these special people in my life. I'll never forget the seed they sowed in my soil. I'll never forget the water they poured in me that caused the seeds to grow.

I'm thankful for the past—I don't celebrate the pain—I celebrate the victories. I celebrate the opportunities I now have to help others. I used the deficits as stepping-stones to success. For once in my life, I am going to define me and change my world.

Yes, people are always trying to spill their water in my lap. They try to ruin my clothes but that old trick no longer works. Everyday I put on "lie repellant" and whenever someone tries to dump sludge on me—it slides right off. Like my kids say "shake the haters off."

There is nothing that will take my joy. My mind is made up. I am a woman of determination. I've overcome too much in my life to care about what others have to say. I have a mission to mend the broken hearted and set at liberty those who are being held captive by their past.

The abuse you may have suffered was wrong. The love you never received was unjust. The rejection you've felt all of your life is not real. You are wanted. You are loved. You are appreciated and accepted. Uh, hello—you're the reason I wrote this book.

Who loves you? Who wants you? Who cares enough about you to inspire me to write to you? That would be God. He created you just the way you are. He loves your quirkiness. He's sorry those people abused you. They didn't do what He asked them to do. They rejected you and they rejected him.

Are you wondering how you can get the water that changed my life? Just ask Him. He has a never-ending supply. He won't try to manipulate you by putting dirty filtered water in a bottle. That's what the enemy does. The enemy tries to sell you counterfeit joy, peace, hope and love. They bottle up lies and place the labels of drugs, alcohol, sex and money on the front. I know because I believed it for a long time. I drank from the sex bottle all of my life only to be left thirsty again—never satisfied.

I know what that feeling is like--searching and searching and never being filled. I know what it feels like for your body to dehydrate. You feel faint from the journey. You long to hear the whisper of an "I love you."

You crave a pure tender touch from someone who claims they love you. You're tired of being used. You're fed up with being abused. You can't live another day with guilt, fear and shame sleeping in your bed.

I know what it's like to despise looking in a mirror. I hated the woman I saw. You want to know your purpose? Do you wonder if things are ever going to get any better? Have you felt like a loser all of your life?

I know how you feel. I've been to that hell but I'm back. There is hope—so don't give up. There is always hope. Hope is a delicious beverage. It quenches every thirst. It heals the wounds of the past. Just in case you were wondering, whatever happened prior to you reading this book is the past. The past is the past. It can't be changed.

I have a love/hate relationship with the past. It's out of my life for good. There are some decisions I wish I could change, but I can't so why worry about them, right?

As I stated earlier, we're born into situations we didn't ask to be in. We didn't get to vote on that. However, you can't allow the past to rob you of a successful tomorrow.

It is time you find out what God has for you. Reject the past and create your future. If you continue to wallow in self-pity over your bad childhood or bad decisions, then you'll always be where you've always been, and that's right where you are. There is a better way.

I'm no different from any of you who have read this book. Your life story may have had more tragedies than mine, but it doesn't matter. What matters is that we don't lie in yesterday's bed.

We must refuse to drink our destiny from polluted wells. Old water carries disease. Make a decision today to stop borrowing water from the lives of others. You don't know the source of their water.

I won't promise days without sorrow. I would be lying to you. And I don't have all the answers. The only thing that I can promise is that God will be there. I can make that promise because I've seen him.

My life could have taken a turn for the worst. I could still be living on welfare, waiting for my next $226 monthly check. I could have more children, been in prison, been homeless. But I'm not. I'm not any of those things because God changed me and He changed my situations. There are no free rides in life. In order for me to reach my destination–my destiny--I had to work to changes

Instead of using negative words and actions as a reason to stay the same, I turned those words into change that would pay for my journey. I had learned to place huge layers of brick around my heart because I was so accustomed to rejection. There was no way that I could fathom the concept of trusting someone or letting my guard down. I wanted to be in control. Staying in control was my way of protecting my heart. But Love had something else to say.

The waters of love and compassion motivated me to see life in the future rather than dwelling over the past. There was no need for that. I couldn't change it anyway.

I could've made excuses. The world wouldn't have blamed me if I stayed poor—it was statistics anyway. Based on statistics, I was more likely to be on welfare my entire life. I was more likely to be poor, uneducated and in one abusive relationship after another. This list could go on and on, but the reality is that I'm more than that.

God brought me a very long way. I would not be who I am if not for Him. I overcame because I got fed up with people defining me. If they couldn't give me clean water, then I'd go create my own. I'd find my own well to quench my thirst and satisfy my life.

You may still be asking "where are you now?" "I'm still here" is my answer. No longer on welfare—no longer a beaten down teen mother—no longer unloved. No! Not at all!

I'm a kind, loving mother, a community leader, a professional, a college graduate, a homeowner, a woman of God and now an author—who would've known.

The trials and tribulations that I endured no longer have a death grip on my future. I refuse to drink the polluted water of insecurity, inadequacy and injustice. I no longer seek fulfillment and purpose through sex, education or accomplishments.

I will never live the life of defeat again.

Life can deal some harsh blows. Either I could lie down and accept them or I could stand up and fight back. Well, I fought back and I won. I won over all the things that people had to say. I won over the effects of the sexual abuse. I won over the abuser. I won over the rape. I won over the rapist. I won over teen pregnancy. I won over the welfare system.

I no longer have to look for love in the wrong places, I see her every time I look in the mirror.

Regardless of the storms that came to drown me out—I'm still here. I look over my shoulders at my past and see that there has been no storm that I've yet to overcome.

So, today I fly high above the criticism and with my face to the wind--I declare that I am that strong, life-watering woman who fascinates the world.

To all the storms that came to destroy me and declared I wouldn't make it--Look at me now!

BORROW WATER?

Never Again...

~ Chapter 12 ~

Soul Water

You can overcome your past. You can lay down all the failures, regrets and fears. You can move beyond the pain of your yesterday and step into a new life today.

Life is about decisions. The decisions you make and the decisions made by others. Decide today to make better decisions. Things don't have to be the way they've always been. Things can be better. Your life can be better. You can be better.

As long as you live, there will be struggles to overcome and hurdles to jump. Trials will be no stranger. Everyone experiences hardships. It's what you do with those hardships that determine your destiny. You can't control what happens to you, but you can control how you respond.

I won't lie to you and tell you the past hasn't affected you. Our past is who we are today. Every mile we walked and every mountain we climbed yesterday created our today.

You have the opportunity and the responsibility to do things differently from what you've learned.

Resistance and opposition are no strangers to me. I've faced this duo throughout my life. I've been abused, rejected, abandoned, and talked about just like many of you. God changed my life and he changed my direction. When you see my past—you understand my Praise... There is nothing too hard for God. There is no one who is counted out. There isn't anyone that He won't love and accept.

You're valuable to him. No matter who you are or where you've been, your life has purpose.

Borrowed Water

In the journey of life we are faced with new walls to climb, doors to open and hurdles to jump. I'm reminded of a track star running the 100-meter hurdles. They run with all their might to make sure they jump every hurdle without touching it. If they come into contact with the hurdle in any way it slows the runner down. It could cost them the race.

I've felt like that runner. I focused so much on jumping the hurdles just right to reach my goal. I could hear some people cheering me on and some chanting disdain. I'd push past the ridicule and find myself moving toward the finish. I'd jump every hurdle with success and cross the finish line.

Instead of feeling accomplished –I'd look into the stands and see the familiar faces of my past. Rejection, abandonment and pain took their places in the crowds—watched my every move and found their way to prove I hadn't come that far at all.

I'd look back at my accomplishments and find myself feeling the same pain over and over again. I'd feel like a failure time and time again. I had come a long way but their presence drowned out the cheering crowds and forced me to worship the ghosts of my past.

The only way I would ever break free was to learn forgiveness for everyone who ever hurt me. It's always been said that "hurting people" hurt people. I say that "hurting people" hurt themselves. As long as I had unforgiveness in my heart, I was never going to enjoy the great strides I made.

Yes, I jumped the hurdles. I even tapped a few of them on my way over and many times they slowed me down. However, I didn't have to quit the race.

I chose to forgive the past and move forward in my new life. It was the best decision I could have ever made. I've closed the door on bitterness, resentment and hate. I could love me in spite of all my flaws, disappointments, failures, successes and triumphs. I could love me just the way that I was.

I was no longer going to allow everything that happened yesterday dictate my joy today and my hope tomorrow.

Enough was enough.

It's now time that you do the same. Forgiveness is not easy. There's pain attached to it, but pain you need to release. If you hold on to it, you won't be the person you desire to be.

Don't allow what others have said or done hinder you from reaching your true destiny. God is the God of second chances. He'll take your pain and turn it into victory. I know because he did it for me. Let him do it for you. God can heal your past, forgive your sins and brighten your future--if you'll let him.

Don't give up on yourself and don't give up on life. Don't allow the decisions of others rob you of the best life you can enjoy today. You no longer have to live on the water of passersby. You can venture out and find life-cleansing water.

I spent the majority of my life living on the water from the mouths of others. I felt like I always had to be strong. I leaned on and trusted in my education, my goals and my accomplishments--all of which never fulfilled me nor gave me purpose.

Soul Water

The best that I could've ever done was to release all the masks and be free. I was created for purpose and that purpose was to have a relationship with God and love me and love his people. God knew every time I soaked my pillows with tears. He knew how I borrowed my identity from what others had to say about me. He knew that I felt like a nothing. He knew how badly I wanted to make a difference in my life and in the lives of others.

There is a great life in store for you, but you'll never get there if live your life looking back. You must keep pushing—keep praying—keep pressing. God can't remove the fear from your life nor can he make you happy. That is your decision to make. You must choose to walk in gladness—choose to smile—choose to sing, laugh, and dance through life. You must choose to have joy in spite of the situations in your life.

Happiness is a choice. It's a state of being. It's the decision to rise above the circumstances and enjoy the life you've been given.

Borrowed Water

Resistance and opposition aren't strangers to me. For the most part we all know what this duo can do to a person. I've taken a drink from their faucet many times only to find my thirst unfulfilled but tainted--Poisoned with every sip.

I've been abused, rejected, abandoned, and talked about just like many of you--filling my glass with one disappointment after another. I knew the consequences of my libation but I continued to drink out of desperation and fear. Sooner of later I had to make a decision to live life my own way.

So, I gave my life to the one that created me. I never gave up on myself because I hate defeat and I wasn't a quitter. Times were hard but having hope was harder. I chose to look ahead in spite of what I saw around me.

Like an oasis in a desert was my vision in my dry journey. God changed my life story and he changed my direction. He was the water that would purify my soul and quench the thirst of acceptance that I had longed for so long.

I realized that there was nothing too hard for God. There is no one that he counts out. There isn't anyone that he won't use to touch lives. I realized that I was valuable to God. No matter who I was or where I had come from--I had purpose.

Many of you may be wondering if you have purpose. As you scan the environment around you small reminders of failure whisper your mistakes and the mistakes of others into your ears. At times you may even question God as to what your position is in life. Where do you fit in? How can you make a difference? Who will make a difference for you?

God knows each one of you and the cries of your hearts. He knows who you are. He knows the number of hairs on your head. He knows the number of your days. He knows what you like and don't like. He knows what makes you cry. He knows what makes you laugh. He knows how your body functions. He knows why it stops working.

He knows when you soak your pillow with tears. He knows your burdens and he knows your fears. He knows when you rejoice. He knows when you succeed. He knows when you fail and he knows what you need. He knows what others have done and he knows how you will overcome.

With everything that happens in life--HE KNOWS. Sometimes our situations don't change, but I know what I know—things are changing. Change takes time. He is doing something even if the something is nothing. If we know that He knows then we should trust--wait--enjoy because the best is yet to come.

No matter what you go through--He knows--He cares--He's working. He did it for me and he'll do it for you.

Remember you can't control what happens to you, but you can control how you respond and you can control how you will live the rest of your life. Don't' allow the water of others drown out your life or hinder your destiny. Always protect your water source. Always dream the impossible and drink the God-inspired possibilities that come.

If You See Her

If you see a little girl who's dirty and un-kept
If you see her with many boys she's slept…
If you see a young girl who's very promiscuous
If you see that her behavior doesn't make sense…

If you see a teenager with a baby on her hips;
If you see her with lust drenched lips'…
If you see her as you pass her in the street
If she smells of lust-scented sheets…

If you see her when you look in the mirror
Have compassion on the person that you see…
For that person had very well been me…

If she must borrow and you must lend
Let the water she pours out not be the water that you pour in…

About the Author

LaToya Brown knows what it's like to make bad choices. But she also knows what it's like to reach her goals. She believes that you can be of no value to others unless you truly value yourself.

Sexually abused as a child, raped as a teen and raveled with rejection and hate, LaToya spent many years searching for love, purpose and acceptance. In her search for these things and more, at the age of seventeen LaToya found herself the mother of three
children.

Though desperate and despondent, LaToya was determined to make a better life for her and her children. In spite of the odds stacked against her, she knew that getting an education was her key to being free from the life that she lived as a child and was living as a teen parent.

Ultimately through God's grace, hard work and education LaToya was able to provide the stability that she and her three sons deserved.

Today, she is a social worker in her middle school alma mater, where she ministers to youth who live the life that she once overcame.

LaToya is emerging as a leader in the social work field and in the community, where she volunteers countless hours ministering to youth.

LaToya Brown is the founder and CEO of ***Soul Water Ministries-Victory Comes In Streams.*** ***Soul Water Ministries*** is an inspirational oasis for those thirsty for God's destiny, purpose and fulfillment for their lives.

LaToya holds a Master's and a Bachelor's Degree from The University of Texas at Arlington and an Associates of Liberal Arts from Mountain View College in Dallas, Texas.

LaToya Brown is a sought after inspirational speaker at conferences, seminars, church retreats, youth rallies and schools

LaToya considers herself to be an inspirational speaker over a motivational speaker as she says that her mission in life "is to inspire others to live past their yesterdays and believe towards their inspired tomorrows."

Latoya Brown's work encourages young women to make positive investments in their self-worth.

LaToya loves spending time with her family and friends, reading a good book, watching the sunset. She honors God for allowing his vision of life and love to flow from her soul into the lives of others.

LaToya lives in Grand Prairie, Texas, with her three children: Tristan, Ashton and JaRicky.

Be KIND.... for everyone you meet is fighting a hard battle...Plato (c. 427-347 B.C.)